A BOY AND HIS TEENS

A Boy
and His Teens

FATHER RICHARD MADDEN, O.C.D.

THE BRUCE PUBLISHING COMPANY
MILWAUKEE

IMPRIMI POTEST:

CHRISTOPHER LATIMER, O.C.D.
Provincial

NIHIL OBSTAT:

JOHN F. MURPHY, S.T.D.
Censor librorum

IMPRIMATUR:

✠ ROMAN R. ATKIELSKI
Vicar General
Archdiocese of Milwaukee
November 9, 1962

Library of Congress Catalog Card Number: 63–13390

(5/66)

TO MY SEVEN BROTHERS WHO,
AMONG MANY OTHER THINGS,
PREVENTED MY BEING AN ONLY CHILD

Acknowledgments

If you're going to write a book about boys, you better talk to girls about it first. Therefore, I am most appreciative of all those teenage girls who were always so ready and willing to offer suggestions on how to straighten out the boys of America. Further, I wish to express my deep gratitude to Miss Cece Bersch who gave so much time and work to this book that it is practically hers; and to Miss Roberta Irvine who so generously helped with the typing of the manuscript.

Thank you, girls.

THE AUTHOR

Contents

YOU AND YOUR GOD

YOU AND YOUR NEIGHBOR

YOU AND YOUR GIRL

Introduction

You're a teen-age boy and so what! Society, in general, thinks you're a bum. Your parents have you going around in circles. If you horse around, they tell you to grow up and act your age. If you try to play the adult bit, they tell you you're too young. OK. Where do you stand? What are you anyway?

So, I'll tell you what you are. You're a man, that's what. Whatever else they say about you, you're all of this. A man. Get it straight. Never forget it. Shape up to it.

Certainly I can understand your being a wee bit mixed up. People call you, and all the guys like you, a lot of things. Let them. Just remember, you're a man.

You are *not* a boy. You have resigned from the "Let's Wipe Out Girls Club." You don't save things any more, like marbles, rocks, birds eggs, matchbook covers, or bottle caps. You have pretty much gotten rid of the camping kick. No longer do you find high adventure invading the local woods, canned beans and raw potatoes flung over your back in a knapsack — beans cooked right in the can, raw potatoes tossed indelicately into the fire, plucked out black as briquets, and bolted down like peanuts, charred, hot, unbuttered.

You don't dig toys any more. The electric train that clattered around the tree at Christmastime has been taken up by your kid brother, and you don't even care. You don't throw tantrums any more. You don't use tears as a tool for wheedling gifts out of your parents. The aimless putterings and wanderings of the boy are no longer a part of your life. Instead, the faint glimmerings of awareness that you are going somewhere have taken over the fringes of your consciousness. No, you are not a boy.

But neither are you a mature man. You are still an idealist. Or maybe a dreamer. Either you're thinking that life is just one big bowl of bananas and it will never change, or you're looking for new horizons because the old ones no longer offer you any challenge or any risk. You can't quite find the handle.

You are yet unaware of the daily Calvary of life, the momentous decisions that face the average man, day after day, in his business career, decisions upon which will hinge complete success or dismal failure. Your vision is narrow. It has walls within the reach of your hand. Your world is your classroom, your clubroom, the corner store, the nearest jukebox, and the girls' academy on the other side of town. No, you are not yet the finished product, and be glad about it. Full maturity will come soon enough. Don't rush it. Your trial by fire is ahead of you. The transition to manhood is rugged. The making of a real man is a cataclysm. So, for the moment, cool it.

What are you? Well, I don't always relish using the word "teen-ager," but that's what you are. You cannot vote. You cannot drink in public bars. You cannot get into those Adults Only movies. You are not able, nor expected, to support your parents. You are not allowed to flaunt the laws.

But you *can* drive a car. You *can* fall into the ugly morass of immorality. You *can* get drunk. You *can* hate leadership and defy authority. You *can* create trouble when you're alone and panic when you're in a crowd. You *can* steal and hate and cheat. You *can* destroy yourself and all of us. You *can* annihilate, little by little, the civilization of which you are a part.

What it comes down to is this. Right now, you can't do much more than look and listen. So keep your eyes and ears wide open; your mouth shut. Learn. Then, later on, you can be anything you want. You can be a hero and a saint; you can be a rogue and an animal. And whatever choice you make will inconspicuously, but profoundly, influence the future of the world.

Whatever we adults feel in our hearts about you, whatever we think, we're still going to turn the controls over to you someday. Because, you see, you are all we have. There is no one else.

We who have preceded you through life will not make any apologies for our failures. We will take no credit for our successes. We will just wrap up whatever we have left, and put the whole mess in your hands.

I like this world. I'd like to see it get better. Not worse. I'd like to see civilization get civilized. And I'd like to think that when we oldsters cop out, we will have done what we could, and then left for you something to carry into the future.

And I like you fellows. I like to see you at your Prom, dressed to the teeth, scotch-tartan cummerbund even, wearing that newly hatched look of all male adolescents. I even like to see you in your old clothes, sloppy as only a young man can be, shoes scuffed and worn down at the heels. And that frail, sick beard struggling for roots. I like being among you. I like seeing you grow up.

But I hate seeing you goof off. I hate to see your lethargy, your indifference, your premature, unfounded cynicism. I hate to see your blithe unconcern for the things of the spirit and the soul.

So, buddy, keep your eye on Christ. Speak and act in such a way as to be assured of His complete approval. Then, although you might not know just where you are right now, in a few years you will know exactly where you're going. And go, you will.

YOU AND YOUR GOD

CHAPTER ONE

It's a Boy

You came into this world just about like the rest of us — practically unknown. Millions of people were not even aware you were being born and, if they were, they could not have cared less. But then you didn't care about them either, so that pretty much evened everything up.

The people who were there when it happened were the only ones that *had* to be there, the only ones that mattered. Your mother was there, naturally. Branded with the curse that God inflicted upon Eve and all women who were to follow her, she brought you forth in pain. She suffered to give you life. Your father was there, too. He was out in that cage where hospital authorities put all expectant fathers, reading everything and anything he could put his hand on, pacing back and forth across the room, smoking interminably, and suffering almost as much as your mother.

The announcement of your arrival was inscribed upon the pages of history. There was no clamor of the mobs at the palace gate, no fanfare or roll of drums. A little nurse walked

up to your father and said so matter-of-factly: "It's a boy."
That's all she said. It was a line she'd used before. She knew
it by heart. She knew it so well and had used it so often the
impact of what she said was lost to her. And yet just a few
moments before, from the depths of God's love and from the
furnace of your parents' love, there had just come forth upon
the earth something unique, a child burning with the fires of
creation; a tiny boy who would one day be able to take in at
a glance the infinity of the skies, whose mind would be able
to assimilate the knowledge of centuries; a little boy who
would live, and then die, only to go on living as long as God
Himself would live, forever. It seems like you might have
deserved a little more notice, rated a little more interest than
the flat stark statement, "It's a boy." But then, what are you
going to do?

In those first moments of your life you were not busy planning your future. You didn't care if the world was at war or
not. You weren't concerned if your parents were rich or poor.
In those early minutes of your life, you knew only one thing,
and you knew it instinctively — you were hungry. So, instinctively, you screamed to be fed.

If you had possessed any consciousness of yourself at that
time you might have, before anything else, thanked God for
the gift of life and for the fact that you were a baby boy, born
in a great country with limitless opportunities for the future
and blessed at the very beginning with the rights and gifts of
an American child.

Because, you see, you could have been something else. You
could have been born one of the teeming millions of a godless
China — and the odds were close because one out of every
four kids born into this world is Chinese. You could have been
born in the slavery of Communism because half the people
of the world are the slaves of Communism. As a matter of
fact, you can be thankful that you are a human being. After
all, when you think about it, you could have been a pigeon

flying around city hall. Some pigeons made it. It could have been you. You could have been a squirrel scrounging for nuts is some city park or a tsetse fly sitting on a banana on your way from Jamaica to New York. I hate to think of all the things you could have been. It's too depressing. The important thing is that you were born a baby boy and it was no accident because God made you. He gave you life. He breathed into you an immortal soul and, when He did, He cut your orders for you. His plan was to let you out on a string for a given number of years and then, when your time was up, to pull you back in. God was your beginning and God is your end. Which makes God pretty important in your life.

Now when God gave you life, He didn't wash His hands of you. He wasn't going to leave you on your own. He figured in His divine fashion that if He let this little nut (you) try to hack it through life on your own, you would wander from the right road and start floundering through the brambles and the thorns. So, for your safety and your guidance, He furnished, through Moses, the Ten Commandments.

The Ten Commandments are not necessarily the name of a movie. Of course, Cecil B. De Mille did make a movie about the Ten Commandments, and he did a pretty good job. Thanks to the advances of science and the movie industry he got more people than ever under the new wide screen. He came up with lots of smoke and fire and plenty of stereophonic sound. But even De Mille missed the profound meaning of the Commandments of God. The Ten Commandments changed the world. Before God blessed the earth with His laws, people didn't know what direction was up. They were nothing but the living wreckage of original sin. Their souls were parched and empty. They were lost.

So when God gave His Commandments to Moses it was His way of saying, "I made you because I love you. Therefore I will illumine your darkness. I will give you ten signposts, ten beacons; follow them and you will never go wrong. They will lead you onward and upward. They will make you worthy of your destiny. However, if you break these laws, if you repudiate them, if you disregard them, you will not hurt Me because I am God; you will only hurt yourself."

God gave you life and then He gave you the map. So now you move out.

CHAPTER TWO

Who's Got the Map?

As you grow older and your interests become more varied, you will slowly develop an awareness that the world is filled with nuts. Day after day you will rub shoulders with creatures who, although they are trying to live their lives the best way they can, are still lost for want of direction.

Everybody is going somewhere. But where, that is the question. Take for instance the oft-publicized beatnik. Formerly he was an engaging nationwide fad; but lately he is being accepted for what he is, and he is on his way out. He is against man. He is against society. He is against law. Against conformity. In an effort to change the world he hates, he creates mediocre art and writes inane, verbose poetry. His personal life consists of moving into his pad, taking the lampshade off the lamp, the legs off his tables and chairs, and his door off its jam. He is one of the night people. Through the day he alternates between painting, writing, sleeping; and through the night he sits around on the floor with his cohorts whiffing the pod (smoking marijuana), worshiping Samoan fertility idols, contemplating his navel, and beating bongo drums — hoping thereby to reach the nebulous state of *nirvana*.

Now, it seems to me that any one of us could achieve the stature of a beatnik. I am sure that if I stopped working and sat up all night smoking the weed, contemplating my navel, quaffing beer right out of the can, and beating a bongo drum, I'd be beat too. Beatniks are looking for something.

They don't know what it is, but they're looking. And as far as I can determine, they aren't having very much luck.

Once, on the streets of San Francisco, I passed by one of these characters. He was garbed in the usual black sweat shirt, blue jeans, and way-out sandals. His beard was twice as scraggy as his hair. The bongo drum was tied to his waist, and he was digging the beat deep by throwing finger snaps around like crazy. I went up to him and, in order to establish some kind of rapport, I said, "Man (for that is what he was), why don't you go home and take care of your mother?" He said, "Man (for that is what I am), like what do I need with a mother? I've already *been* born." I would call this confusion. Beatniks are so mixed up that occasionally one or another of them will do a brody off the Golden Gate Bridge because he just can't make the scene any longer. We can't call them evil. We can call them lost.

Even in the so-called normal classes of society, we still find lost souls foraging around for some purpose in life. Take for example, a town like Palm Beach, Florida. It is commonly known that Palm Beach is a haven for the wealthy. It is a place for spending the winter. Beyond that, it is also a refuge for Yankee failures. People who have botched up their lives in the North migrate eventually to Palm Beach. Save for the solid citizen, the well-formed family elements, Palm Beach is a resort for the divorcée. Everybody down there, it seems, every floater is divorced. If you're not, you begin to feel that you don't belong. The usual thing down there for these lost people is to pair off in some bar, get stoned, then stagger down to the beach with a blanket for the purpose of playing kissy-face on the sand. If you happen to be wealthy, you can do better than a blanket. Your butler will follow you with a Persian rug.

Those who are concerned with the spiritual regeneration of Palm Beach will say to me, "Come down here. There's all kinds of work to do." But I don't know. As a priest you have to expect losses, but not *all the time*. Down there it's all losses.

All the summer resorts of our nation — Miami, Las Vegas, the beaches of the east and west coasts, the mountain resorts — these places are all filled with people on the search. And it is just too bad. I am very wary of calling any of these people bad. They are not necessarily that. But they are swept up in doubt and they are perplexed. They are looking for the right road. Which is not an easy thing in view of the fact that there are so many wrong roads.

All the wrong roads are basic variations of three main ones. These are the roads that lead nowhere. These are the roads that arrive nowhere.

First, there is the beauty road. Everybody wants to be beautiful. Having a beautiful form has been beamed upon America as the best way to achieve fulfillment. Women spend two billion dollars a year on beauty aids, 75 million dollars alone going for lipstick. And men are spending their share for beauty aids too. Women are expected to have a perfect figure. If God doesn't provide it, then some girdle company will. A woman is no longer permitted to be real. She must be painted, powdered, perfumed, and packaged in a foundation garment. Men are no less guilty. In society today a man is not permitted to sport a fat, happy tummy. He is forced to have heart attacks from workouts at Vic Tanney's or is condemned to eating health foods and drinking diet juices. It's only too bad that we cannot be content with the way God made us. It's too bad that we are committed to driving ourselves crazy taking care of a carcass that doesn't have long to survive and will ultimately rot away in some lost grave where a sign reading "Perpetual Care" is lost in the tangle of weeds and tall grass.

The second road is the money road, and man indeed walks this one. Strangely enough, in spite of how much money he makes, man is always broke. He spends everything he makes. He can never make enough to satisfy his hunger. Often enough, the more he makes the less content he is. Money might bring luxuries, but what it provides in this category it takes away in another. Money is often the direct cause of the destruction of man's peace of mind.

The third road is the trinket road. We're almost neurotic in our efforts to have every kind of new material possession that is put up on the market. Every time we get something new, we tire of it and begin looking for something to replace it. The merry-go-round never stops spinning. And once you're on it, there's no getting off.

Like everybody else you young men must move. But before you do, know where you are going and how you are getting there. Watch out for the dead ends. Watch out for the roads that lead nowhere.

CHAPTER THREE

The Real Treasure

For a while there, I was romping all over the country throwing a battery of questions at teen-agers wherever I found them. I discovered that girls generally like the color blue, Old Spice, and tall men; but they hate nail-biters, cigars, and mustaches. They like cigarettes and whisky sours but are repelled by large diamonds on men's fingers and poor grammar in their mouths. They expect their dates to help them on with their coats, to open car doors for them, to dance well, and to hold hands as they walk together along the highways of life. They rarely read *Life* and *Newsweek,* have rather vague plans for their future, but are counting on having about five or six kids before they die.

But you young men aren't so fussy. As far as the girls go, you dislike loud talkers, pixie haircuts, and vulgarity. You like a girl who knows how to fix her eyes properly, who wears black pleated skirts and white blouses, and who isn't overly expensive when you take her out.

All this, of course, proves nothing except perhaps that we all have different views and opinions on just about everything and we're ready to talk about them. The only thing we have in common is this: we are all searching for happiness.

It doesn't matter what we do, we are always aiming in this direction. No one deliberately tries to make himself unhappy. Even if some guy has a persecution complex and is always arranging to get himself nailed to a wall so that he can cry, it is this very misery that makes him happy.

The quest for happiness is a basic instinct within us. We yearn for it. Yet, if we take a casual gander around us, we will find many unhappy people and they are unhappy because, although they are riding their hobbyhorses, they keep missing the ring. They try looking for happiness in the wrong places, and not finding it there they end up in a heap of frustration.

The whole thing seems pretty simple. The only happiness, the only real happiness, can be found in being what we are supposed to be and in doing what we are supposed to do, namely, fulfilling the purpose of our existence.

You know what this is, too. When you were little boys in first grade, you might have been pretty dumb in a lot of things. You might have flunked sandbox, milk, and nap, but you never forgot the purpose of your life because some good little nun drilled it into your empty little heads. The reason why God made you is that you might know, love, and serve Him, so that you might be happy with Him forever in heaven. Anything else that you might do with your life is quite secondary to this. The depth of your happiness on this earth will be in proportion to the effort you expend in getting to know, love, and serve God.

So what about this? What about, first of all, knowing God? Well, let's face it. Whenever anybody mentions God you immediately create a picture of Him sitting on a golden throne with a long white beard looking down at the world, but a wee bit too old to do anything about it. So let's not use the word "God" here. Let's use the word "Christ."

Do you know Christ? If you don't you're missing out on something. I mean you're *really* missing out. But how do you get to know Him? Well, how do you get to know anybody? You ask questions about him. Like, in religion class. Yet, the picture of high school boys' religion classes is a very dull and glum one indeed. The impression you leave is that the whole session is an absolute drag. If you go to a Catholic high school, you have to be in class and you are bored. If you're getting your religion one hour a week through the Confraternity of Christian Doctrine, a lot of you aren't even showing up. Your attitude toward religion makes it pretty clear when we look at you, that all you want is out, and fast. You will never really know Christ unless you read about Him, unless you study Him. And if you don't know Christ, you will never find within you the fire to combat sin.

It is pretty obvious that those of you who are always looking for an opportunity to cut corners and always asking how far you can go without committing a sin, it is pretty obvious that you are the ones who know nothing about Christ. This intimacy with Him, which you should cultivate, is the one thing that could change you from some kind of a doped amoeba into the militant, struggling, battling soldier that you should be. You have to look into His life. Then by way of knowing Him better, you speak to Him. This means the developing of a life of prayer. Daily contact with Him. Brief conversations with Him. No kidding, some of you have about as much prayer life as a bent snow shovel.

With the knowledge of Christ comes love of Christ and with this love comes a brand-new sparkle to your existence. It's a new kind of love. Not love for your parents or your family, not love for your friends, not love for your girl. But a love for Christ. It is the one love which, if it is absent, leaves an inconceivable emptiness in your life. Nor is it the kind of love that is proven by talk. We can say we love Christ, we can shout it from the highest building, but the proof of our love is in the third factor, service.

Service of Christ does not involve any extraordinary activity. He put it so plainly himself when He said, "If you love me, keep my commandments." Serving Christ means, quite simply, doing only those things that you know He would want you to do; speaking as He would want you to speak. Serving Christ means tearing out of your lives everything that is ugly and mean and vicious and immoral. It means, in effect, that the life of Christ is perpetuated in you. Does it sound too far out, too fantastic? Is it too much for you to give? Well, if it is, then you are a misfit. You are bungling your chances; **you are failing to fulfill the purpose of your life.** And when you fail in this, when Christ is no longer important to you, then, boy, you can look for happiness for the rest of your life, and the only thing that life will ever dole out to you is a big dry handful of ashes.

CHAPTER FOUR

Worse Than Death

Recently a Princeton college boy came up with the very astute observation that "the whole world stinks, but it's the same all over."

Regularly, if mankind is not involved in a worldwide war, then a lot of funny little dictators and a lot of funny little people get their own little wars going someplace. Somebody must call a meeting and assign each little country a specific time for its own little war.

Every time you read the morning paper, you are advised that somebody got his in some bar last night. Maybe a gas station or a drugstore got knocked off. Or some kid kills off his best girl because she got some crazy notion that they shouldn't go steady anymore. Maybe some nut carried a bomb aboard an airplane and — Boom! — confetti. Always somebody is divorcing somebody. Yes, each morning the world bares its soul across the pages of our newspapers. There is a sickness there; a deep, creeping, evil strain in the blood of man.

We read about these things and over our coffee cups we analyze and psychoanalyze, we weigh and balance, we add and eliminate — all the time trying to find a reason for it, and possibly a solution. We blame one another. Parents and children blame each other. Democrats and Republicans blame each other. Catholics blame Protestants and Protestants blame Jews. And Jews blame Catholics and Protestants together. Everybody is trying to finger everybody else as being respon-

sible for the pestilence of our times. You hear words like dis-
graceful, dishonorable, criminal, and inhuman. But actually
and simply, you can wrap up all the evils of our time in one
package and explain all of them with one word: sin.

Sin is an unfashionable word. It is a word that is disappear-
ing for lack of usage. New words are replacing it. A man
who murders his wife is not sinful. He is sick, we are told.
A fat teen-age boy beats up his skinny father, but he is not
sinful. He is misguided. The divorce machine that turns in
ever widening circles is not sinful; it is merely an "unhappily
married person's right to happiness." Gross sins of impurity
are merely labeled "release from tension" and theft is sloughed
off with "I was underpaid. The company owed it to me."

You can call sin anything you want, but you can't change
its complexion. It is still found at the roots of most human
tragedies. War is a result of greed, which is a sin. The persecution of minority groups, whether on religious grounds or
social grounds, is the result of injustice, which is a sin.
Juvenile delinquency, in most cases, is the result of divorce
and remarriage, which is a sin. Some man's poverty is usually
the result of another man's avarice. Because we can say that
sin is at the bottom of misery, so also we can say that if
everyone followed the teachings of the Gospel there would no
longer be any such thing as human misery. Of course, we
would still have our floods and ravishing fires, our volcanoes
and tidal waves and earthquakes; but these would be piddling
problems. The great enemy of society today is sin. And every
time you commit a sin you help chop your own legs out from
under you.

But the greater tragedy of sin, by far, is that it cuts you
off from your God. When you are in the state of sin, you
lose your pipeline to heaven. You are on your own. You say
to God in so many words, "You go Your way and I'll go mine.
You make Your laws and I will make up my own." Where

does this leave you? Well, it is hard to imagine just how desolate it leaves you.

For instance, your mother becomes very ill. The doctors have done all they can. You stand there and look at her in her pain, teetering between life and death, and your first impulse is to fall on your knees and beg help from the only source possible under such circumstances, God. But, if you do, you are only wasting your time. In the state of mortal sin you can do no morally good act, you can achieve no merit for yourself or for your mother. She has to go it alone. If she counted on your help, your prayers, she made a mistake. You can't help her. You might run into some church and drop a dime into a box and light a candle but you're just wasting your money. In the state of sin, the only prayer you can offer is the prayer for forgiveness. Other than that, brother, you are useless.

Mortal sin is an act, not only of open betrayal and rejection of God; it is also an act of rankest ingratitude. Judas wasn't the only one who kissed Christ on the cheek. You're no different when you commit deliberate mortal sin. Christ, the best Friend you will ever have, asks one thing of you, but you choose to do the opposite, something else. By this, you become the victim of the greatest sin of all — the sin of pride. You think you are big enough, self-sufficient enough to live your own life. By rejecting His laws you prove that you think that your own laws are better. You turn Christ out of your life, and you let the world of sin in. The pleasure of sin is small recompense for what you have lost; because when the chips are down, and your life has run its course, you have nothing. Christ is gone forever and the world you chose in preference to Him slowly and surely crumbles and turns to ashes in your mouth.

I mentioned before that beauty, money, and material possessions cannot of themselves bring happiness into your life. Sin goes one step farther. Not only does it fail to bring happiness (maybe some momentary pleasure, but never happiness), but it serves up a large portion of eternal misery.

So if anyone asks you what the greatest evil in the world is, you know it now. Mortal sin. And if it is a question of choice between mortal sin and death, never forget that death can only destroy your body, but mortal sin can destroy your soul. And nothing, absolutely nothing, in this whole big world is quite as hopeless or irreparable as a lost soul.

Bucket Mouth

You can't comprehend it, nor can I; but there was a time once when the only thing that existed was God. There was nothing else. Just big, almighty God. He never had a beginning. And if you find that hard to understand, remember it is a lot easier to believe that God never had a beginning than to believe that He *did* have one. Then, for some reason known only to Himself, God decided to start making things.

Now we've been to the movies, and we've seen pictures such as "I Was a Teen-Age Axolot" or "The Monster from Outer Potrezebie." The plot is old and comes in three parts. One, the mad scientist creates this monster, see. Two, the monster runs around terrorizing pretty girls, old ladies, and the country in general. And, three, the monster finally turns on the scientist, carves him up with a jagged edge of an old broken test tube, and is then rubbed out himself by the combined forces of the army, navy, marines, and Boy Scouts of America with first-aid kits on their backs. They make a big scene out of the monster doing in his maker. You can count on the monster coming on strong in this scene, and it's ok too, because those mad scientists only get what is coming to them.

But God as our Creator deserves more. He has a right to our devotion, our service, and our love, and He doesn't always get it. As a matter of fact, if you take a good look at man, you can't help feeling that when God created man, He created some kind of a monster. And in typical monster fashion, man has repeatedly turned against his maker.

God made trees and the trees are real nice about it. They grow leaves for God each spring. God made cows and cows are going along with God by giving milk twice a day and staying contented. But when God made man, He borrowed headaches for Himself. When God made man, He outdid Himself in generosity. He delved deeply into His treasure hoard and came up with something of His own image. It was God's finest hour when He made His finest creature — man. But man has forgotten his maker. Like you do, sometimes.

I'm not saying you're a complete ingrate. After all, we Americans give God a place in our society. True, His name is not mentioned in the Constitution, but it is mentioned in the Declaration of Independence and the Articles of Confederation. Most of our presidents have been God-fearing men who publicly called upon God in national crises. Lincoln, with his immortal "that this nation under God shall not perish from the earth," set a standard for presidential conduct.

The name of God is solemnly invoked in our courts of law. And every day at high noon when the Supreme Court convenes, the crier, among other things, chants: "God save the United States of America." The name of God is found in our Pledge of Allegiance. It is found on our coins. And if you ever have a chance to take a good look at a dollar bill you will find the words *annuit coeptis*. If your Latin isn't so hot, it means, "He has favored our undertakings."

America as a nation holds the name of God in high respect. It is a tradition of our forefathers. It is the public image. But what about the individual? What about you? I'll say this much. Some young men don't have much respect for anything when they open their mouths. They don't seem to care what comes out.

George Washington, besides chopping down cherry trees and crossing rivers in open rowboats, also wrote letters to his troops. And in one such letter he told his men how much he regretted the habit of cursing and swearing that was becoming so prevalent in the continental army. But he didn't know how bad things really were, or how bad they were going to get.

Some fellows have such foul mouths that it's a wonder they are able to eat with the same mouth they talk through. What is all this talk anyway? I'm not saying vulgarity is always sinful, but I am wondering what kind of Brownie points you are trying to make when you use it.

Does a dirty mouth make for greater manliness? Certainly not. It tends rather to turn a man into a boy. The filthy mouth is just a weak-sister substitute for solid character. I've met a lot of successful businessmen, and I believe they are successful and have gotten along because they have always spoken as gentlemen. And gentlemen have clean mouths.

Is cursing or swearing effective in any way? Not at all. Suppose your golf ball ends up in a sand trap just below the green. Try putting your nose right down on the sand-locked ball and damning it from one universe to the other. You know what will happen. Nothing will happen, that's what. Cursing won't get the ball up on the green. Only a good steady nine iron. And in the same vein, you could tell a friend to go to hell, but I doubt if he is going to run right down to some travel bureau to check schedules. Cursing and swearing among young men is just a rotten habit. So let's get on the stick and clean up the language.

Your reputation for being able to turn a room blue with your language not only brings disgrace upon you personally, but also upon your family, your church, and your school. Above all, reverence the name of God. Have respect for the name of Jesus. Don't go bouncing these holy names all over your little world. In other words, God made you. Love Him. Don't turn into a monster. We have enough of them already.

CHAPTER SIX

An Endless Calvary

I have it figured pretty close, so I know that I am just about old enough to be your father. That means I'm plenty old. I am so old I can remember a five-cent hot dog, an eight-cent bus ride, a two-bit haircut. And in my memories of the olden days, I can still recall how Sunday used to be a rather special day. All the bars were closed tight (still are, as a matter of fact, in Philadelphia), and there were no movies. Sunday was entirely different from the rest of the week. It was God's day and everybody seemed to realize it.

Mass was a big production for the whole family. So was the breakfast that followed. Benediction in the afternoon was fairly common. Then at night we listened to Fred Allen on the radio because, believe it or not, there was no television.

Things are all shook up now. Sunday doesn't belong to God any more. It belongs to the people. The weekend has become the center of our life, time for the big gorge and the running revelry. Things have become so bad that, of late, one very misinformed, misguided, and confused Protestant minister was quoted in leading magazines as saying that the Lord's day should be shifted to Wednesday, so that church obligations would not interfere with people's weekends. Brother, this is where I get off.

Setting aside Sunday as a day of special worship of God is pretty much up to you as an individual and to your family as a group. I don't want to be dictating to you young men, but I do wish that you would start throwing yourselves into the breach by fighting those forces that are trying to push

God right out of the picture on Sundays. And you can do it.

I would ask you to make every day of your life God's day, but God Himself only asked one day a week. He's always so understanding. What I do ask of you, absolutely, is Mass on Sunday morning (or afternoon, if you just can't get the old bones going earlier). I don't care if you've been up all night Saturday and awaken Sunday morning feeling like a sackful of doorknobs, Mass is a must.

We priests manage to work ourselves into just about any kind of a job. We have become scientists, psychiatrists, social workers, educators, laborers — everything. But then, so does everybody else. Anybody might be any one of these things. But no matter how you look at it, the priest is a priest for only one purpose. It is not, primarily, to preach, to hear confessions, or to baptize. The one basic reason that a man is made a priest is to offer sacrifice. Or simply, to say Mass. If he did nothing else in his whole life but say Mass, he would still be fulfilling the end of his priesthood.

So, you see, the Mass is important to us. We aren't obliged to say Mass daily, but it would be a rare kind of priest who did not look forward to this privilege each morning, and Mass for us is a privilege, not an obligation. The priest's whole life is centered around the altar. He takes the world joyfully with him as he ascends the altar steps. He engages in the great give and take of the Holy Sacrifice, when at the Introit and Oration he speaks to God; and when at the Epistle and Gospel, God speaks to him. He goes to God through the Offertory and God returns to him at the Consecration. It is this living, moving drama of the Mass during which we priests, as the most privileged of men, can hold God in our hands each morning. We think this is pretty great.

But priests aren't in this Mass thing alone. This is not our own private devotion. The faithful are in on it too. All of us, priest and people, gather around the banquet table of an altar and offer the holy Sacrifice together. To have Mass without

a priest is impossible; but for a priest to have Mass without
people is sort of ridiculous.

But what do you think about it? This is a question we'd like
to ask people when we see them gathered in church on Sunday
morning. We wonder what the gang of fellows think about the
Mass as they slip out the door during the sermon to grab a
quick smoke. We wonder what the woman thinks about hear-
ing Mass as she strives valiantly to hang on to the end seat
while everybody else goes crawling over her. We wonder about
the teens who horse around during Mass, fooling with their
prayer books, or spinning their rosaries back and forth around
their fingers. And all the others staring around, waiting for the
finish so that they can get back home again.

Congregational singing or not, general participation or not,
some kids are still backing off, letting themselves out of what
should be one of the most meaningful experiences of their lives.

We ought to do something about this. Surely those attending
the Sacrifice of Calvary today should not repeat the demonstra-
tion of the mob on the first Good Friday afternoon. On that
day, Christ looked down from His cross and saw His execu-
tioners shooting crap for His clothes; the soldiers marching
back and forth, holding back the crowd, hoping He would die
so that they could get back to their barracks; the politicians
daring Him to come down from His cross; and the whole crowd
of morbid curious sightseers. It must have been a very discouraging sight to Him as He hung there dying for them.

In general, let's begin making Sunday what it should be,
the Lord's day. We spend six days a week occupying ourselves
with the things of men; let's spend one day occupying ourselves
with the things of God. Then, when Sunday evening comes
along, and you have been piously with it all day long, you can
sit back in a big soft chair with a coke (or whatever else you
are given to drinking) and watch the late show on TV without
having any regrets for having cheated God out of His just
due on Sunday.

CHAPTER SEVEN

Help at the Rail

The human race is filled with weaknesses, and since you are actually a part of the human race, you have your weaknesses too. Some of you are so apathetic, so lacking in drive and enthusiasm, that it's a shame. All you want to do is lean up against the wall with your hands in your pockets, shoulders hunched, bored look on your face, just waiting for the bomb to fall so that you might be delivered from your misery. Some of you are lazy. Every time you see a chair, your posterior faints. There are some among you who think about girls too much (like all the time), drink too much, and study too little. As far as some of you are concerned the world could just go off somewhere and hang and it wouldn't faze you at all. There are many things wrong with you, but then there are many things wrong with all of us. But one thing I have always admired about you is your deep-seated sense of loyalty. Whether a cause be right or wrong, true or false, if you are loyal to it, you are really loyal.

Now if we could direct this loyalty along godly lines, if we could only channel this loyalty toward Christ, then all your other faults would just wither on the vine as you grew into manhood. But it's just the old thing of getting to know Christ better.

It has always amazed me and, to tell the truth, annoyed me to notice how far back we men lag in our devotion to Christ in comparison to that opposite sex which we must contend with. I give a lot of youth missions around the country and, invariably, the girls at the mission outnumber the boys three to one. Not only are there more girls, but they seem to have a deeper awareness of the presence of God and prove it by their conduct. In giving some of these missions, there were times when I had to physically eject boys from church. Some of them came to the mission drunk or under the influence of narcotics or they were fooling around in church as if they were in some theater. The only reason some of them were there was because the girls were there. So out they went on their "kazazzas." But I have never found myself throwing out any girl for lack of proper conduct before the Blessed Sacrament. What's wrong with us fellows?

Some people have tried to explain away the churchgoing habits of men. They say women find a strong emotional outlet in religion. They enjoy their religion. They love the atmosphere of church. They get a kick out of praying. Maybe so. But this doesn't explain everything. When Christ died on His cross, it wasn't in a church with candles burning, the scent of incense in the air, the gentle coloring of stained-glass windows reaching across the floors. It was all horror and blood. And yet, when you might have expected his men friends to be there, they proved themselves quite gutless and were hiding in the hills or in upper rooms around town frightened to death. But there was no lack of devoted women around the cross. They were women and therefore they were frightened. But because they were women they were there at the foot of His cross.

I think it is a crying shame that men make, and always have made, a much poorer showing than women when it came to serving Christ. If a girl can make a daily visit to the Blessed Sacrament on her way from school, I see no earthly reason why a boy cannot do the same thing. For if any boy would drop into a church and take a long searching look at what was a perfect Man hanging on His cross, I am sure he would be the better for it. Are we calloused? Don't we care? Are we indifferent to the price Christ paid to redeem us? Don't we think we owe Him something? Well, I can't answer that, because I don't know. But I will insist that our service is a pretty shoddy one and we ought to do something about it.

Take, for instance, the incomparable mystery of the Holy Eucharist. Here again the girls always outnumber the boys at the rail. How do we explain the male apathy to the living presence of Christ in Holy Communion?

Repeatedly, you young men have complained about how hard it is for you to be good. You have used the silly argument that because you are basically weak you have to stay weak. But the answer to the battle for soul survival is the very thing you avoid — the abiding presence of Christ that can only come to you through Holy Communion. I don't kid myself. Just because I'm a priest is no guarantee that my soul is saved. So I am at the altar each morning not to show off, not to impress anybody. I'm there because I need God, and it is just as simple as that. And if I didn't have God then I wouldn't be hanging in there very long.

The lack of young men at the Communion rail means one of two things. You are in the state of mortal sin and unworthy to receive Communion, and this is horrendous; or you just aren't interested, and maybe this is even worse. You can't explain away your absence at the rail with the trite old line, "I am not good enough to go to Holy Communion." Boy, you think you're so humble. Well, get it and get it straight. It is not the truly humble man who sits in the back of the church and never goes to Communion. The truly humble man is the man at the rail. He is publicly admitting, "Dear God, I am a bum and the only way I will rise above it is with Your help." But you, who stay in the back as far away from Christ as you can, whether you know it or not, you are silently admitting to the world, "I don't really need God. I can get along without Him."

Our dear Lord doesn't want to listen to all your incantations of unworthiness. He left Himself on this earth for you. What He wants is your worthy and grateful acceptance of His finest gift, the gift of Himself in Holy Communion.

Men are supposed to be practical. We're supposed to be thinkers. We're not the bundles of emotion that women are. We are not creatures of intuition. We are men who can see things clearly. Therefore, we must plan for the future, and the rail is a good place to do it. For when the priest gives you Communion, he says, "Body of Christ" and your respond, "Amen" — your testimonial of your faith in Him and your love of Him. Then you are planning for the future, the one big important future — your eternal happiness.

CHAPTER EIGHT

A Magical Invitation

I think, by this time, you young men are aware that I am a priest. And you are right. I have been one for a little over twelve years, and I have papers to prove it. I have never labored in a parish or served in the foreign missions. I have baptized about ten children, married a half-dozen couples, taught for two years in a minor seminary, filled the position of vocational director for my Order for three years; and for the rest of the time, I have been giving high school retreats and youth missions all over the country. What I have done and what I have not done — this is not really important. What is important, and I have mentioned this before, is that each morning I offer the Holy Sacrifice of the Mass.

When I was ordained on a cold December morning in 1949, I said to myself, "Priesthood, I love you." And I tried to prove it. I was in the sacristy putting vestments on fifteen minutes before Mass was scheduled to begin. I took the Blessed Sacrament morning after morning through the tangled traffic of Washington, D. C., just to bring Christ to those who were too sick to come to church. I blessed anything and everything. Put it up in front of me and it got blessed. With both hands, even. Yes, on the day of my ordination I said, "Priesthood, I love you." But I didn't know this priesthood, so how could I love it? You have to know something before you can love it. I only *thought* I loved it. But I just didn't know.

Now I know. Now, after almost 20 years of looking back, I

think I can honestly profess this love which I have for my vocation. Because there are no longer any secrets about it. I know the joyous side — the constant abiding awareness that, when men are in the state of mortal sin, I am the only friend they have. I am the only one who can forgive their sins. I have had addressed to me countless thousands of times the reverent "Good morning, Father."

But I know the other side of the coin, too. I have had unbelivers, in fits of bigotry or ignorance, spit at my feet. In a family of mixed faiths, I have been damned by some members of the family for bringing the consolations of the Last Sacraments to other members. Often I have been very, very tired from my work in the vineyard. Often I have been discouraged at the sight of those vast fields, white with the harvest of souls, and so few around to reap them. It has been my overwhelming privilege to lift fallen teen-agers from the gutter. But as I did, I knew that when I moved on, in my never-ending role of circuit rider, some of them would slip back again, and there was nothing I could do to prevent it. I have worked with young hoodlums, trying to give them a vision of what they could be. But their futures were determined. They would return to the environment that spawned them, and there, some day, they would die in the street with a policeman's bullet in their hearts.

Maybe you have to be a priest for fifty years to know what it's all about, but, after twelve years, I think I get the picture. I know the joy and happiness of being a priest. But I also know the loneliness of Christ and the disappointments of Christ. For to be a priest means to share this with Christ.

How did it all start? When does a kid start becoming a priest? When you were ten, you started serving Mass. There was the long walk to church to serve the six o'clock Mass, and the silence of the dark streets softly shattered by the milkman and his clumping horse making their early rounds. Then the big, quiet, almost empty church, and the tiny bell you controlled, and the smell of sour Mass wine. Maybe this was a start.

You didn't grow up in any valley of peace. Jews, Negroes, Poles, Italians, Irish — all managed periodical clashes on the battlefield that was your neighborhood playground. Not with guns or knives. Nobody could afford them. But with fists; and, in extreme cases, with rocks. And your own thinking in the thick of the melee: "Just what are we fighting for anyway?" Later on, exposed to minor vandalism for the first time, and to petty thievery around you, the thought erupted in your mind, "This just isn't right." And on into the middle teen years and all around you, your friends pairing off into gruesome twosomes, indulging in the new-found pleasures of the flesh, unaware of the insidious leprosies spreading in their souls. And your own soft thought: "Somebody ought to help these kids."

So you make the big move. You decide to become a priest. You find some vocational literature, look at a picture of a gang of monks, all smiles of course, hiking along some country road. This gets you and you sign up.

When word leaks out through the neighborhood about your newest caper, your trial by fire begins. Your buddies are badgering you to "hang around another year anyway, and we can have some more kicks." Older people, in that dangerous way they have of creating doubt in budding vocations, wonder if "perhaps you aren't just a little young yet to know what it is all about." Soon you begin to get the idea that everybody has grave reservations about your vocation. Everybody, that is, except your folks.

Anyway, you get busy a few weeks before your ETD, buying the stuff you're supposed to bring along with you. And as the days pass and the time runs out on you, you begin to suffer pretty big doubts yourself. Thousands of them, day and night.

Then, it's good-bye time. First, over to your girl's house for a last piece of cake and a glass of milk. There is this feeling that because you're going to be a priest you automatically are holy or something, so you kiss your girl good-bye with only one lip. Finally, good-bye to your folks. Right there, you'd like to die. You'd just like to die. You wish that you had never even thought about a vocation.

You take your last look at the world, and one thing you know. You're not leaving this world because you don't love it. You do. Maybe that's just why you're going. And you are not leaving this girl because you don't feel that you could have ever really loved her. It is simply because you have found in Christ a greater love — and you have to be honest enough to admit it. So you leave the world because Christ asked you to leave it. You follow Him because He asked you to follow Him. And when you do, you become in some way like Him, a savior of the world upon which you turn your back.

In the monastery they take your blue suit, your money, your cigarettes, and your freedom. But after a few months, when the plague of homesickness has fled, and you have fitted into the smooth-running machine of monastic life, you wonder what was with all the qualms before you joined. You toe the mark, do what they tell you, watch the clock, and before you know it, you are on your way to the altar to receive the holy oils of priesthood. You have run the gauntlet, you have achieved your dream. And now, thrown into the battle for men's souls, you find yourself with only one lingering question: Who will take my place when I'm gone?

I manage to do a lot of milling around among high school students, and repeatedly I am thunderstruck at the rough diamonds and unrefined gold I find there. This is the kind of raw material from which the Master drew His first Apostles. This is the stuff the world needs. But the big question bugs me: "If so many of these kids have what it takes to be great priests, why are so few of them coming through with it?"

In asking these young men why they did not want to be priests, I received many strange answers. Or, rather, excuses.

There was the boy who told me he didn't want to be a priest because he was the only boy in his family and felt an obligation to carry on the family name. I asked, "What's your name?" He said, "Walter Bozzniack." Like the world couldn't survive without a Bozzniack. Or the lad who didn't want to be a priest because he didn't like Latin.

There were all kinds of reasons, freely and sincerely given, but only a few of them had any real validity to them. Generally, their objections fit into three categories.

The first category was, "My parents are against it." This is a sad indictment against the Catholic parents of today, one for which they shall some day answer to God, but a kid usually can't fight his parents so there's no point in even talking about it.

The second category was, "If I join up, I'm afraid I might quit." These kids are still waiting for the direct line to heaven. They fail to understand that nobody ever walked through seminary doors with any assurance that he would still be there tomorrow. There is just no way of knowing "for sure." You have only the gentle promptings of grace. You go into the seminary, do your best, and leave the rest to God and the seminary authorities.

The third category (and the most common) was, "I love the world too much." This includes, primarily, the social life, dances, parties, and the opposite sex. These lads labor under the false premise, "If you love fun, stay in the world. Priests never have fun." Really, I don't think I need point out how utterly ridiculous this is. Any young man who never possessed the capacity for laughter or fun would be a poor bet, indeed, for any seminary.

So the call is out. The magic, magnificent invitation, "Come after Me," is on its way. And lucky indeed is the lad who hears it and answers it. For his is the world, and his is the kingdom of heaven. There is a frightening lack of priests. You are needed. Don't miss the boat. Check it out.

CHAPTER NINE

Away for the Weekend

You don't know why you're doing it. You're such a busy guy. There are so many things you could do this Saturday and Sunday. You just can't afford a lost weekend. But you set yourself up for it. You had to go and open your big mouth when some retreat leader invited you to make a retreat. And you can't back out now. They'd nail you to the wall. That's the way guys are.

Then, again, everybody seems to be making retreats these days. And you hate the black looks they give you when you have to admit, "No, I never made a retreat. What is it?" The stare they give you! They make you feel like a leper. A retreat, if nothing else, will get you on the offensive. You'll be like everybody else.

So you decide definitely to go. Maybe the weekend will be a real blast after all. A bunch of your buddies, spending a few days together away from those complicated, confusing women in your lives, where you can let down your hair and talk straight man talk. Be away from it all.

You won't need many clothes, so there'll be room in your overnight bag for a box of candy, a few packs of butts, and a new deck of cards to liven up the party (or whatever they call it) on Saturday night. You secretly hope the stakes won't be too high.

Right off, you like the retreat house as you enter it on Friday night. It's big, expensive, plush; just the kind of a joint you'd like to own some day. You like your room. The chatter

with your roommates is breezy; laughter comes easily. Just
as you kick off your shoes, the dinner bell hustles you to the
dining room for your first meal. It's good.

From there you are swept along with the crowd into the
common room for briefing. Here, finally, is where your world
caves in beneath you. The first announcement is one on silence
— no talking until Sunday afternoon. Your bile rises. Your
face blanches. You suppress an urge to fling yourself to your
feet in protest. But everybody sits there and takes the news
like a gang of dummies. What can you do?

What are you going to do for conversation? What about
the party Saturday night? How can you have a party in
silence? And in the midst of your spasm, the priest is up there
trying to make his point. He's explaining silence. He's trying
to tell you that the greatest thing that ever happened in this
world happened silently. Creation itself was just the breath
of God. Bethlehem was silent. So was Calvary. And today
the steps of God across the world are silent steps, and if
you're making a lot of noise over the weekend you just won't
hear God when He walks into your heart.

Gradually, all this begins to make sense to you as the
graces of the retreat begin taking over. You forget about the
deck of cards in your bag and the date you broke for Saturday
night. You decide to test yourself and see if you really can
keep your big mouth shut for the next 48 hours.

Then, upon the scene, comes Father, the retreat master.
You look this guy over. You check the shape of his head and
the size of his shoes. If he is a barefooted monk, you watch
his toes in fascination. How lumpy are they? How pretty? How
many? Yes, you look him over and you are not too sure you
like him. He's too old. He must be all of forty. He's probably
out of it and will snow you with a lot of spiritual gobbledy-
gook that he stole out of some old musty book of theology.

He starts talking. You like him less now. He annoys you,
this little man. He's talking about things you don't even like

to think about. He wants to know what you are doing on earth. And your soul, what provisions are you making for its salvation? And the big statement that slaps you right across the face is the one about dying. How you hate that kind of talk. Who wants to die? And yet, what about it? How long do you think you can live? Everybody's dying. It's easy. Why, every time you climb into a car, you take your life into your hands. Yes, what about dying? What will you say to God when you meet Him face to face?

And as if all this isn't bad enough, this little man with both eyes on heaven had the crass gall to call you a phony. Imagine, you, a phony! Well, you are a little different inside than you are outside. You do like to make the big impression. You hide your weaknesses. You blow a big horn when you give to charity. You lie, gossip like an old biddy, sow seeds of dissension. And you have no respect for another's reputation. You have two hands, one for warm clasps of friendship; the other for sliding dirks into enemy backs. You go to Mass on Sunday because it is something you have always done. But a phony? Well, maybe he's right. You could do better. Thinking too much of yourself. Never giving anybody a decent shake. Always, "What can I get?" instead of "What can I give?" Yep, phony is the word. No doubt about it. And with this, you are ready to make the best retreat possible.

You go right to bed that night. No horsing around. You have a lot to think about and you do it with your rosary in your hand. Soon you're asleep. Asleep and snoring. All night long your roommates are throwing shoes at you. But they don't bother you. You're asleep and snoring!

Yes, the retreat changes you. Before you leave, you will see things differently. You will never again attend Mass the way you used to, kneeling there like a dumb spectator killing time. Now it will be different — an actual participation in the Sacrifice of Calvary. *Christ offering Himself again! Christ offering Himself forever upon the altar.*

And when you go to Communion, it won't be with a swagger but in deep humility because the great God of heaven and earth is now about to make you a part of Himself. You have made the best confession of your life. You have cleared up your doubts and anxieties. You have developed in you a prayer habit that will change you from a talking Catholic into a doing Catholic. You, buddy, are a new man. The weekend speeds by so quickly that, when Sunday afternoon arrives, you are surprised. You are surprised at how fast the time has gone. You are surprised at your new outlook on life. You are surprised at the many opportunities that were found to improve the world. You are surprised at all the love of God that had lain for so long, buried and unused, in your heart. And that new deck of cards. This is the big surprise. Still in your suitcase — unopened!

CHAPTER TEN

Your Little War

Teen-agers are always big news. As subject for conversation among adults, youth rates equal time with such matters as sex (any conversation usually gets around to this), religion (spoken with studied and guarded care so as not to be offensive), politics (you have to have definite views here or the conversation will revert to sex again), and money (mostly pay envelopes and stock markets). Therefore, whenever I appear at a gathering, sex is skirted ("Father is a priest, you know"), politics is avoided ("We don't know how Father votes and he won't tell us either"), money is no issue ("Father has a vow of poverty and knows nothing about it"), and religion is dropped ("If we give Father the ball, he might run right through us"). The only thing left to talk about is teen-agers; and all adults have definite ideas about you young people.

I come on real strong when adults blanketly condemn youth. I like to use my little knife in pointing out that most of the evils of today are not the fault of youth. It takes more years than kids have accumulated to be the proficient sinners that some adults are. I do not subscribe to the belief that all the fads kids cook up are a threat to the moral fiber of our national structure. But I am forced to agree with people when they accuse the younger generation of lacking proper respect for lawful authority. Because, when they talk about this, they are not whistling *Dixie*.

Juvenile delinquency is hardly more than a mass revolt of youth against authority. This revolt (and there is a little bit of the revolutionary in all kids) can be best illustrated by what a kid once said to me, "I only wish there didn't have to be a Sixth Commandment." Now this slays me. Here is a kid of some intelligence (you would expect) who is seeking release from God's law. Here is a young person who, in a quest for some kind of idiot freedom, blithely expresses the wish that God had not given us Commandments, for then the little creep would be completely free.

Well, if we reject the Commandments, we'd be free all right — free to destroy ourselves, free to leave the protection of God's loving hand for the savagery of a world without God, free to break our hearts and twist our souls into pretzels, free to seal ourselves off for all eternity from Him who said, "I have come that you might have life."

If this is the freedom you want, you can have it. For myself I'll take the joyous slavery of God, and the comforting shackles of His law; for only the discipline of God's laws will eventually lead to the freedom of living with Him forever.

Leaving God for a moment, we can also detect this youthful aversion to authority in your attitude toward policemen, principals, teachers, and even your priest. Anybody who might slow you down, anybody who might frustrate your plans to swing without restriction automatically goes down on your list. This is all bad enough, but when you turn your guns on your parents, you're making the biggest mistake of your life. When you begin to look upon your folks as enemies, then you utterly destroy our faith in your intelligence. Unfortunately, youth today does not credit parents with much intelligence. But maybe that situation is not new. As a matter of fact, it is old stuff.

When I was sixteen, I didn't think my parents were with it at all. They were good parents all right; parents didn't come any better. They meant well, I figured. But they were old. They were of another era. They just didn't understand modern kids. The life we were living was just too fast and too vastly complicated for them.

Now, many years later, I realize what a pompous little fool I was. My parents didn't become smart all of a sudden. They were always smart. The big shocker of the year, as far as you young fellows are concerned, is: parents are always smart and rarely wrong.

Looking back, I wonder if I will ever be able to forget the hard times I gave my folks. I wasn't exactly a delinquent, but I did blast off into orbit once in a while. I can easily forget the times I was good; I only wish I could forget the times I wasn't. Just think, before anything else, they gave me life and thereby made it possible for me to become a priest. Now, they could have decided, in the face of hard times, to have only two children and, since I was the third kid, I could have ended up somewhere out in the vast reaches of eternity. I would never have made it to earth. This fact alone humiliates me for not having been a better son.

Your own folks are no less good. They made sure you were well fed and well watered through the years. They always arranged their budget to provide that your clothes were a little bit better and a little newer than their own. They watched through the night when you were sick. And whenever you disgraced them, their hearts broke because of it.

I think there should be a lot more peace treaties between you and your folks. Recently I was part of a little true-confession session being carried on by four girls, all high school sophomores. One of them in tears said, "But my mother is so mean." And her friend, by way of offering some consolation, said, "But Mary, all mothers are mean." Now this jazz I just can't dig. I violently contest the statement that all mothers are mean.

Therefore, let's do a little bit of shaping up on the home front. Instead of bleeding your folks of every conceivable trinket and treasure, and of every possible nickel, you should take the measure of what you owe them and come across with your debt. First of all you owe them love which, under ordinary circumstances, should be a very easy thing to give. Then, you owe them respect. It doesn't matter how much money they have or how fine their clothes or how broken their English, they are your parents. Be proud of them. Also, you owe them some assistance. Working around the house is no disgrace, nor is it below your dignity. You don't have to look very long or very hard to find things that could be done and should be done by you. By all means pitch in and help. Finally, you owe them obedience. For you they are the voice of God. When they speak to you, God speaks to you. When you please them, you please God.

So get out that white flag, bury the hatchet, and start trying to get along a little better with your folks. Indeed, they are not perfect and they have their faults. They can make mistakes. Anyone can. But being obedient to your parents is a sure solid way of doing what is right; disobedience is always dangerous.

One final thought. Take good care of your parents now. They are only on lease to you. Some day God will take them away. It is not a nice thing to think about, but on that sad day when you stand beaten and overwhelmed with grief at the side of your parents' graves, I only hope you have no regrets for having helped put them there.

CHAPTER ELEVEN

The Life You Save

Today, with so many married couples not wanting to have any kids, the big problem is not dying. That's easy. The big problem is getting yourself born. A lot of kids just don't make it.

But we did. We're the lucky ones. As long as we have managed to find ourselves here on earth, let's manage to stay a while. Let's protect our own lives as well as the lives of others. Some eggheads don't think life is very important (other people's, that is). They are worried about the earth becoming too crowded. We call them "Malthusians" because they are adherent to the theory of Malthus, a man who reasoned that, since the earth did not increase and people did, there was a problem. The only solution, the Malthusians figure, since we cannot do anything about making the earth larger, is to get rid of surplus people.

As a matter of fact, the earth will never be overcrowded. The population is unequally distributed, that's true; but this isn't nature's fault, or God's. It's man's fault. Our East Coast is overcrowded to a certain degree. You can stand on the top of the Empire State Building and, beneath the reach of your vision, there is 10 per cent of all the people in the country. It leaves a lot of open space out west.

And the worldwide picture is interesting. Japan is the same size as Montana. Montana has only one half million people. Japan has ninety million. Just what we are going to do about this, I leave to other people to decide. What I am trying to say is that there is still plenty of room left on this earth.

Another factor which disturbs our Malthusian friends is the astronomical advance of medical science. Diseases which formerly destroyed life have been rendered quite powerless. And some day cancer will be conquered. Fewer persons will die. But Malthusians need not worry. As long as we have madmen behind the wheels of automobiles, plenty of dead pedestrians will litter the streets of America. Dead, too, will be many madmen behind the wheels of their cars. And we do manage to come up with a war occasionally which levels things off a bit. Let's not worry about there being too many people on this earth. Let's work to protect and save the ones we have.

Indeed, it is a precious thing, this life of ours. To preserve it is one of the basic instincts of our nature. A man can be suffering agonizing pain on his deathbed, but he is alive. And he prefers life with its agony to death with its uncertainty. Nobody wants to die. Everybody wants to go to heaven, but nobody wants to die.

There is no doubt about it, some day all you young people will throw that big seven because dust is a must. As soon as we are born, we begin falling into an open grave. But there is no sense in rushing things, for ourselves or for others.

Thank God the ordinary teen-ager is not running around looking for lives to snuff out. The average boy is not like the one that I visited through prison bars. I look at him through the iron grating and I said, "So you had to go and kill a woman." And he said, "OK, Padre, so I burnt the old dame. I didn't mean it." But whether he "burnt the old dame" or "cooled her" or "starched her," it all adds up to one thing. Murder. And it's a dirty word.

It's good that we are a little more civilized today than in the days of the Wild West. Back in that time I wouldn't have been marshal of Dodge City for any price. I would have never taken Paladin's job. I just wouldn't feel right or safe with everybody in town toting a 40-some-odd. The thought of it gives me the creeps. I'm glad that stuff is gone. True, many hoods carry switchblade knives on them, but chances are you have never seen a switchblade knife or a zip gun. Mass murder in our streets and hopped-up lynching mobs are old hat. It just isn't so easy to get murdered any more. And that is grand news.

You young men are, I'm quite certain, opposed to murder. But there are many of you who are not adverse in any manner to a good street rumble. Unnecessary rumbling is dangerous and often serves little purpose. True enough, there are occasions when a fight is unavoidable.

When I was a kid I didn't exactly like fights, but I liked to win them. And in my neighborhood there was no way out. You had to fight. The playground up the street was always crawling with young undesirables. And an undesirable was anybody who was using the swing or the basketball that you wanted. A few blocks farther was the local swimming pool. If you wore your good clothes to this joint, you came home in a barrel. So you wore rags. The place was plagued by young thieves who went, like voracious little crickets, from one locker to another, lifting anything that wasn't nailed down, as well as anything that was. In order to save your money, your clothes, your self-respect, you had to fight. But we fought for one reason only. We fought because we were kids.

Mature, grown-up people (like you're supposed to be) have no real cause for battle. The only adults who fight are drunk anyway, and don't know any better. Maturity and civilization, as well as the teachings of Christ, demand a better system for solving problems.

There has been just too much fighting in the world as it is. Just imagine, from the year 1496 B.C. until A.D. 1861 there were 3130 years of war and only 227 years of peace. That means that in the course of 3357 years we have had 14 years of war for every one year of peace. And things haven't improved any since 1861. We're great fighters. We're also children, in this respect.

Christ wasn't making like a joker when He blessed the peacemakers. He expects each one of you to buttress society by the force of your gentleness and your love. He doesn't need the violent upheaval of your tempers. We can all do without that. Establishing peace within the relatively small circle of your influence requires strong moral discipline. The Sacraments should take care of this. It also requires some external show of peacefulness, and it is surprising how much your clothes for instance reveal your attitude toward peace or war.

The average hood, by virtue of the clothes he wears, seems to indicate that he is spoiling for a fight. His black leather jacket with lots of phony chrome and the slag drag to it, his tight-fitting britches with a reat pleat, his fruit boots (or stomping boots, if you will) are all marks of his pugilistic tendencies. His feminine hairdo which makes any barber wonder, "Does this guy want a haircut or an oil change?" is the mark of the troubleshooter with strong pansy leanings. Briefly, he's a jerk acting tough.

In other words, if you're men, dress like men. Put away your battle gear. Get out of those silly suits of armor. And then perhaps there will be a lot less struggling, battling, and fighting in this world into which Christ tried to bring the beauty of an enduring peace.

CHAPTER TWELVE

Light-Finger Lester

Just about the only place in the world, outside of Russia, where you can be robbed blind, and like it, is in a monastery. Of course, you don't have to like it, but you do have to accept it. And I know what I am talking about because I have lived in a monastery for a long time. Our vow of poverty creates this situation. It prohibits private, personal ownership. So it comes down to this: If you don't own anything, how can you lose it? No one loses what he does not have.

The powers that be tell us that we all have an equal share in the wealth(?) of the community. Everything belongs to everybody. But they don't kid me. Common ownership means simply that you end up with nothing. Brother Somebody is using your typewriter. Brother Whoziz is using your razor. And the Superior is blowing his big "bazoon" into the nice Irish linen handkerchief that your Aunt Gladys sent you for Christmas.

But monasteries are different worlds. Systems that work there could not work in society. Therefore, common ownership, while great in a monastery, would be disastrous in society. In the world, private ownership is the thing, and it is a basic tenet of Catholicism. What a man honestly acquires, whether he buys it or works for it in the sweat of his brow, is his forever, unless he freely relinquishes it.

That is why stealing is so wrong. It violates a man's sacred right to that which he has honestly acquired. And let all thieves remember that a successful hoist doesn't make the loot automatically yours. It never becomes yours, not in a zillion years. The old theological axiom always carries the day — a thing always screams out for its owner.

Some day, everything might go black and you'll find yourself driving around in a hot short with a furnace and a band. (In the language of the trade this is a stolen car with a heater and radio). It will never be yours, no matter how long you keep it. It constantly cries out for the one who really owns it.

Therefore, let's not be Light-Finger Lesters. The kleptomaniac is around, but he is relatively rare. This is the guy who when he sees something, anything, he has to steal it. He might hate watermelons, but if a watermelon truck goes by, he steals a watermelon. He has to. But what do we do about the ordinary healthy teen-age shoplifter who steals simply for kicks or because he doesn't want to work for the money it takes to buy?

For one thing, lock and safe companies are up to their ears in sales. Factories and warehouses are equipped with burglar-alarm systems. Locks are found on all doors and windows. Floorwalkers are always on the prowl in our supermarkets. Society is trying to protect itself from the thief; the thief is invading our homes and places of business. The war is on.

In one year young thieves, breaking and entering, cost the city of Chicago $400,000. In Baltimore, 2029 school windows were broken by young vandals. Many of these kids were never caught. A cat burglar shinnied into a New York home, latched onto a $15,000 piece of jewelry, slid down the rainspout, and slipped into oblivion. He was never caught. Other shady voyagers, masters of their trade, are cracking safes and heads, robbing and plundering, and getting away because the cops can't get all of them all the time.

The only thing left, therefore, as a sort of deterrent to these clever artisans who are daily plucking the feathers of honest people, is that moral stricture known as "restitution."

If what they say is true, that there is a little bit of larceny in all of us, then restitution is a word that does indeed make us wince. It means that there is no such thing as a perfect theft; no such thing as getting away clean. Any thief must buck the percentages. He risks capture and a jailhouse gown if he gets caught. If he doesn't get caught, he still faces the law of restitution which requires that he return what he steals.

No, there is just no point in laying siege to the fortress of other people's property or possession. That's why I repeat this — shoplifting is so ridiculous. You go into a dime store, you lift some Persian Melon lipstick at the cosmetic counter, or a cake of soap, or the latest Chubby Checker record. The management might not catch you, but God does. And as long as you live, you are in debt to that store. It is a debt that never evaporates or disappears. It is always with you. There is no escape.

The sin of theft is never really forgiven until you both confess it and then promise to make restitution. Actual restitution, or at least the sincere desire and unfaltering resolution to make it as fully and as soon as possible, is necessary in order to obtain complete forgiveness of God.

So restitution is the only hope I have of getting back the Mickey Mouse watch that was stolen from me when I was in the fourth grade. I am still waiting. I will probably wait forever.

Most of us are ordinary people with many, many needs. I *could* tell you, if you do not have all the world has to offer, then steal. But this would be wrong. If you can't come by something honestly, go without it. Because, under the circumstances, you will be happier and safer without it.

CHAPTER THIRTEEN

Worth a Smile

I'm tired of being conned and cheated and swindled by every guy that comes down the pike. I have been sold clothes that fell off my back, appliances that never worked, and watches that never kept time. I'm sick of all that. So I'm turning over a new leaf. From here on in, I'm going to be perfectly honest. How about joining me? How about making this one of your patterns of living.

Naturally, I'm not going to lose my head. After all, I must continue to use prudence and discretion. I must still avoid certain issues. I cannot bring myself to be so cruel as to tell at all times the absolute truth on all occasions. For instance, suppose I am approached by a rather large (plain "fat" is a better word), unattractive, middle-aged woman who has a problem. She is looking for a husband. For her, it is open season on men. For her, every season is hunting season. Her problem: "Father, just what is wrong with me?"

Now, if I wanted to tell the absolute, unvarnished truth, which means revealing exactly what is on my mind, I would be forced to say, "You want to know what's wrong with you? You really want to know? Well, I'll tell you what's wrong with you. First of all, you are much too fat. You look like you're following yourself. You have a figure like a bag of walnuts. This is the only thing that is really wrong with you. So stop eating so much and do a few calisthenics." This is what I would be thinking, but I couldn't say it. I would end up sweetly answering her, "Well, you might try dropping a few pounds. You might also take pains to make yourself as physically attractive as possible. This, along with your naturally wonderful disposition (what in the world do I know about her disposition?) should do a lot for you." Whew! But this is not really dishonest.

Furthermore, I think I shall continue to smile and be nice at banquets. I don't think I'll let people know how I feel about these things. To be honest, though, I couldn't begin to tell you how much I hate banquets. I've been riding this banquet train, following this peas-and-carrots circuit for a long time now, and it keeps getting worse, it never gets better. Once in a while you hit a good one. In the past nine years I have spoken at only one really good banquet, at the Elbo Room in Palm Beach. Outside of that, nothing. Ordinarily the food is bad enough. But all during the meal, notes are being passed among the big people, messages are being carried about by a whispering courier, and I don't know what it's all about because nothing is happening anyway. The jokes of the toastmaster are old and not funny. But the crowd laughs because, after all, he is one of them and he is doing his best. Then, when it's time for me to speak, I'm just as lousy as the rest of them. We should have all stayed home, that's what. But I think I shall go on making the scene, telling the banqueteers what an honor it is to be there, and that this wonderful, successful affair is something that I shall never forget (for sure). After which, the kitchen crew comes in and we all clap, and then go outside and throw up. Anyway I don't know why I'm telling you my problems.

To get back to this thing of honesty, whatever business you go into later on, be honest. The business world could use a little honesty. I'm not saying it's all crooked, but a lot of it is tainted.

You have all been exposed to the big store downtown with the screaming, garish signs plastered all over the windows: PRICES SLASHED. FORCED TO SELL. EVERYTHING MUST GO.

WE'RE CUTTING OUR OWN THROATS. WE'RE GIVING IT
AWAY BECAUSE WE LOVE YOU. It's a great show and it's
worth a smile as you walk by. But I hope you realize that this
guy isn't going over the hill to the poorhouse next week. In
fact, for every shiny new fluffle that you carry out the front
door, he's hauling two more in through the back door. This
system isn't all wrong. You're getting exactly what you pay
for — junk. The whole thing is just a gimmick to snare the
sucker.

Now don't get the idea that you are not allowed to make
some money in business. Of course you are. A real-estate firm
will sell your house for you, but they aren't doing it for kicks.
They have a right to their cut. They earn it. A jeweler will
sell you a watch for $75 even though he bought it himself
for $40. He's not cheating. Even a large fund-raising company
will approach your pastor with a deal, "We'll raise a million
dollars for your new school as long as you give us 5 per cent
of the whole ball of wax." This is business.

Likewise, you are not dishonest if you manage to fall into
some kind of a deal where you can make money without
even getting out of bed. For instance, when I was a kid I made
a deal with Ralph's Grocery Store to deliver circulars around
the neighborhood for 35 cents. I grabbed a bundle, went
home, asked my younger brother if he wanted to earn a
quarter. He took the job, got the two bits and I'm home free
with a dime. No sweat. This is using your brain; it is not dishonest. What would have been dishonest would be taking
the money, then chucking the circulars down the sewer. And
don't think it wasn't done in those days. The sewers were always clogged with circulars.

Kids were dishonest then; kids are still dishonest today. In
these days a teen-age girl will take money for a baby-sitting
job and, for all she cares, the kids could drink poison or cut
their heads off. Because the baby-sitter, is too busy on the
sofa with her boyfriend. This is dishonest — not to mention

the sofa bit. Other teen-agers can't sit through an examination in school without cheating in some ingenious way. This is dishonest.

When it comes to dealing with your fellowmen, let's get back to the Golden Rule. "The way I want this bird to treat me; that's the way I must treat him." Remember, the patterns of living and the habits you develop now are the ones that will stay with you for the rest of your life.

CHAPTER FOURTEEN

A Size-Ten Mouth

Whenever anybody said "Crime doesn't pay" to Nick Romano, he just laughed because to him it was one big, fat, happy joke. His dedication to the questionable causes of dope running and bootjacking (robbing drunks who staggered alone out of Chicago nightclubs and juke mills) was paying off. And handsomely too. He went in big for expensive sport jackets and slacks. He wore the finest shoes. Crime, indeed, wrapped glad rags around Nick's corporeal envelope.

Crime doesn't pay? Phooey, figured Nick. He developed his own philosophy of life, "Live fast, die young, and have a good-looking corpse." He was 21 when he discovered, after murdering a cop, that crime doesn't pay after all. As for his live fast routine, he did. He lived very fast. And he died young. Very young. But there wasn't anything good-looking about his corpse after they put the juice to him in the electric chair.

There is no point here in trying to figure how Nick got that way. Maybe, as a young boy, life was cruel to him. Maybe life hurt him. So he declared war on life. He would strangle it, crush it, take everything from it he could, then throw it away like so much garbage in the gutter. Perhaps if he had tried putting something into life, perhaps if he had decided to do something worthwhile so that other kids might get a better deal than he got, maybe then he would have turned into something acceptable to society. But he declared war on society. He lost.

In this jungle we call life, we cannot very well remain passive. We must either love or hate. Nick hated. He paid the price of his hatred. Our obligation is to love, for love is far more rewarding, far more fulfilling. Loving your neighbor has many facets and many tints to it. And one of the important phases of this love of neighbor is respect for the next guy's reputation.

When I was a boy, I was struck down by automobiles twice, almost drowned once, fell out of innumerable trees, and on one occasion almost smoked myself to death on a box of old cigarette butts. After all that, I'm lucky to be alive. Furthermore, I'm glad I made it through those hazardous years of childhood. I'm glad I'm alive. I think life is pretty precious. We all do.

But a reputation is as precious as a life. A man with a reputation and no life has some kind of a problem; but a man with a life and no reputation is really up against it. That is why destroying a man's reputation is almost as bad as destroying his life. And sometimes much more painful.

I remember well a convert coming to the monastery one day and saying, "I have only three friends left in this world. You and a Jewish couple who are pagans. When I joined the Church ten years ago, I was given to believe that its members had love for one another. I found out they don't. My reputation has been so torn to pieces by Catholics that I am forced to leave town. And in leaving town, I am leaving God and I am leaving the Church. It has all been a bad dream!"

The only addition I can make to this is simply: if this man never finds his way back, some very unkind and uncharitable Catholics are going to answer to God in strict justice for their crime.

It is sad, indeed, that a reputation, which takes so long in the building, can be destroyed so quickly. And some people are masters in the destruction of others' reputations.

A destructive word, cast lightly upon the winds of life,

can rarely be taken back or explained away. Trying to remake a reputation is like smashing open a pillow in a strong wind and then reclaiming all the feathers. It's quite a job.

And this old saying you might use, "Well, after all, it was the truth," only makes things worse. If you tell a lie about somebody, you can run around admitting you told a lie. But if you tell the truth, that's it. It's all over. The truth really hurts.

Your reputation is important to you. Other people's reputations are equally important to them. Let's respect one another. You don't take any shots at other people, they don't take any shots at you.

And for heaven's sakes, in the name of charity, learn to keep your mouth shut. Some of you young men are just like these girls who will get on the phone and say to their girlfriends, "I promised that I wouldn't say anything about Gert unless it was good — and, believe me, this is good. This is really good." Here she is, the human vacuum cleaner, going around scooping up little morsels of scandal and then casting the bag to the wind. Somebody should really lean on her type.

What is this strange, nervous urge that comes over us the minute we are entrusted with a secret? What is this obsession to reveal what has been left with us in deepest confidence? We just can't seem to keep our mouths shut. We're like these electronic IBM computers that pour out information as fast as people pour it in. We have to talk.

Like the lady who says, "What's the use of suffering, if nobody knows about it?" Charles Lamb grabbed the essence of it all when he observed that one of the greatest satisfactions he ever enjoyed was to do something good in secret and have it found out by accident.

The classic pattern for keeping secrets can be found in the priest and the seal of confession. A priest might break his heart, but he will never break the seal. He might make many mistakes, but never this big one. Never, even in the face of death, will he reveal secrets left with him in that dark box.

When someone lets you in on a secret, true, there is no such imposed seal. But the keeping of that secret should be no less sacred. Abuses are so numerous in this department, loose gums so common, it seems the only way to keep a secret is to tell nobody. Absolutely nobody.

But you say, "Oh, I'm only going to tell my best friend." Remember, your best friend has a best friend, and his best friend has a best friend. So when you wake up the next morning, everybody in the world knows about it.

Let's all check ourselves on our ability to keep a secret. And if we must honestly admit that we can't be trusted, then we should have the common decency to wear a big sign on our backs: "I am a blabbermouth. Don't tell me anything."

Let's earn the reputation for being kind and compassionate. Let's not get dragged down into the morass of idle gossip, detraction, and all the rest of the ugly ilk. If we give others a break, we will get it back. As the poet says, "There is a destiny that makes us brothers. We cannot live our lives alone, for whatever we put into the lives of others always comes right back into our own."

CHAPTER FIFTEEN

Your Uncle Sam

Catholicism, friend, is rough stuff. Some religions might be geared to make people feel good inside, but Catholicism is a challenge to the highest and noblest aspirations of a human being. It requires not only perfect love of God and perfect love of neighbor (which you already know), but perfect love of country (which you might have considered as mere patriotism). Perfect love of country carries the edge of sanctity. Good Catholics should automatically be good Americans.

We Americans are proud of our flag. We boast about our "American way of life." We enjoy unlimited freedom. We face no obstacle in our quest for "life, liberty, and the pursuit of happiness." These are the privileges which we gladly hold to our hearts. Yet, we should no less gladly accept the obligations that come with the privileges of American citizenship.

Take taxes, for instance. Most of you don't pay taxes yet; but your time will come. Always remember, paying just taxes (and our taxes are just) is a serious moral obligation. Yet, the screamers and the complainers are always sounding off about this. Look, when your folks pay their taxes, they are not pouring their dough into a bottomless pit. They are not giving away their money. They are buying a share of America. The beautiful (however deadly) highways that you ride on, the best in the world, were paid for with the American tax dollar. Your state parks with all their recreational facilities are the beautiful result of taxes. Schools and universities even.

So when you start paying taxes, pay them joyfully. It's considered an obligation; but, actually, it's a privilege.

Then, another obligation which, by virtue of your faith, you owe your country, is this thing called military service. Here again the congenital gripers come forth with their inane rantings because "our boys must subject themselves to the draft." Our country happens to be strong today because of a lot of young men who gladly paid this particular debt to their country. Some of them paid the highest debt possible. They paid with their lives.

So I feel no sympathy for the mixed-up guys who are out burning their draft cards. They say they are only exercising their right. But get enough guys doing this, and soon there won't be any rights for any of us, because there won't be any freedom for any of us. It should be the shining goal of all mankind to achieve peace; but if half the world insists on toting guns and preaching conquest, then the rest of us better not stray too far from our own weapons.

I feel very strongly about this particular matter because I have strong military leanings. Recently, when my plane landed at the Seattle airport, Father Tom McIntyre, Chaplain for the 325 Air Wing, was there waiting for me. Now I wasn't looking for any big military reception — just an ordinary staff car to whisk me off to my destination; but when I had to maneuver my big frame into his tiny tin can on wheels (made for midgets more than for people) I suffered a few grave misgivings about the coming week. On this note of doubt, we started off for McChord Air Force Base to bring down thunder upon the earth during what the Air Force calls "The Annual Preaching Mission." (Too bad the army and navy cannot make provision for the same type of thing.)

Now I am just a plain, old civilian and I figure my piece of cake is teen-agers, not air-force personnel. So I was about to become Mr. Amazement. The first thing that struck me as we approached the front gate of the air base was the tall handsome Negro airman on guard there. Resplendent in air-force blues, with white stock and shoelaces, he gave us a crisp wave-on; then, recognizing the car as that of an officer, he came up with the most beautiful high-balling salute that I have ever seen. Right away I got the idea — "This place is on its toes." But this was just the beginning of a long week of amazing sights and amazing people.

Stronger than anything else, perhaps, is the feeling of preparedness that permeates the air around you. Maybe the military is a red-tape jungle, I don't actually know; but it seemed to me that everybody knew where he was going and what he had to do. Down on the flight line, I watched the base commander, Colonel Donovan F. Smith, bring in a 106 jet fighter like it was a feather and I said to myself, "Even the big men are Go." The whole thing makes you worry less about Russia. It gives you a nice contented feeling that if trouble does come, we have the men who know how to handle it.

A few weeks prior to this, I had been associating with teen-age boys who were in trouble with the law for stealing hubcaps; but here in the air force, teen-agers were carrying the full responsibility for the perfect performance of the jet fighter and for the life of the man who flew it. Some of you teen-agers might be goofing off these days, but not those in the air force. They are youthful giants. And the parents who have given them to the country need not worry about their becoming men. They are men already.

One factor that is outstandingly clear is the proper place that God has within the Air Force. I am not contending that every individual is a God-fearing man, many are far from it, but to the mind of the Air Force, man is composed of body and soul, and each is given proper consideration. This attitude makes the work of the chaplain immensely easier. Parents need have no fear that the spiritual lives of their sons and daughters in blue are being overlooked or neglected. As a matter of fact, enthusiasm for the mission, as borne out by attendance records, reached a far higher peak than a comparable mission in some civilian parish.

The chaplains are on the ball. And here is something else the civilian might learn from the military. Nowhere else have I found clergymen of all faiths working together in greater harmony. Racial prejudice does not exist in the Air Force; neither does religious prejudice. Many times in the course of my week on the base, I sat with different chaplains of different faiths and felt the glow of rapport. They were all men struggling to keep God where He belongs, and whatever personal differences we felt, they were not considered important enough to cripple the integrity of our joint efforts.

Indeed, life on an air base is a life of its own, vastly different in so many ways from civilian life. Families who live there in base housing have their own way of looking at life, their own codes, their own particular privileges and problems. Each night as I was falling asleep, I hear the sound — and so did many fearful wives — of giant 124's churning down the runways and up into the dark skies on their way to some distant country; and hours later when I was asleep — but probably not the wives — these heroic young men, who put their lives on the line every day, were out fighting the raging elements of sky over one ocean or another. When I left McChord, I wanted to say thanks to all these men. I didn't know how, of course. But I can only hope that in some manner they will discover how much we appreciate what they are doing for us and for America. When your turn comes to slip into the ranks of the military to help in the preservation of our freedom and our peace, you can be assured that I'll be there to thank you too.

CHAPTER SIXTEEN

The Killer Kick

It only takes about one second to have your head chopped off. "So what," you say. Well, all I am trying to say is that it is a lot easier to die for Christ than it is to live for Christ. But live you must. And grow up you must.

Right now your folks think you're idiots. They're sure that you will always be idiots. So in order to stem the inevitable, they are always giving you advice. You hear it all day long. "Open your dirty ears and listen. Keep your feet off the table. Clean your fingernails. Stop gargling peanut butter. Get out of my sight. Stay home. Get up. Sit down. Go to bed. You're just like your father. Study. Move. Come home. Scram. Jump. Work. Drop dead." No kidding, your head's spinning. So let me add a couple more words of advice.

Don't drink so much. Man is an ingenious animal. No matter where he lives on this earth, no matter what kind of material he has on hand, he will always find something and some way to make booze. But just because he makes it, you don't have to drink it all. You guys make me nervous. You don't say, "Let's go out and get a beer." You say, "Let's go out and get smashed." Go easy on the sauce. You'll grow up a better man and you'll live longer and happier.

And here's something else. Drive carefully. The greatest majority of the accidents in our country today are caused by teen-age drivers. You're going too fast. We're not against speed, as such. It's the roads. They can't take the kind of action you want. Slow down. Play it safe. And remember, the life you save may be some beautiful blonde's, and we need them.

Now, here's the big one. Be on the lookout for narcotics. If you see any, run. Maybe you have never had any personal contact with the problem of dope and its victims, but the thing is very real and it is spreading.

Last year, in Brooklyn, the police collared a nineteen-year-old "pusher." They found sixteen capsules of heroin in a cigarette package in his pocket. They also found out that he had two apartments, a closet full of two hundred dollar suits, and a flashy car. This fellow boasted that he made as much as three thousand dollars a week selling narcotics to school kids, all of whom had to steal money some way to keep themselves in dope.

This is no spook story. It is real enough. If you haven't come face to face with it, count your blessings. I've seen it. I've seen the results of it. One day I was with some cops in a large eastern city jail when they brought a young addict in. The poor kid was the picture of agony and despair. His face looked like a stepped-on Halloween mask. He was screaming for a "fix." In such cases the police will give him one and then gradually wean him, cutting down on it until he is without it completely. The doctor got a needle ready, but the kid wanted to give the stuff to himself. So he took the syringe from the doctor and plunged it right into his stomach — a real mainliner. It was quite a sight.

All the results of dope addiction make you kind of sick, especially when the "users" are just kids. They have usually been tricked into the business. Some "pusher" will talk them into trying a "reefer," just for kicks. This is marijuana in the form of a cigarette. Although the kid is always sure it will not go any further, his die now is pretty well cast.

After a while, he becomes interested in something bigger, something that will satisfy him more. Automatically he is led into using heroin, a vicious drug taken from morphine. This has a certain tranquilizing effect, but he gets a craving so intense that the victim will commit any kind of criminal act, even murder, to keep himself supplied.

When a kid finally gets himself hooked, he not only becomes an outcast of law-abiding society; he becomes a reject from the underworld itself. He has served his purpose. He has filled the coffers of unscrupulous dope pushers. Now, when he can no longer come up with the money for a fix he is thrown aside. His insatiable appetite for the stuff has made him forget all else — his God, his church, society, law, and his eternal destiny. He is, tragically, alone with himself. He is just about the most miserable human being alive.

Once a "junkie" starts pouring heroin into his veins, he becomes a kind of wild animal. He is a threat and a danger to society. He wakes up shaking and sweating, his body pumping with a terrible demand for the "snow." He has lost all sexual desire and all human respect. The only reality is his "contact," the man from whom he gets his "flat" or his "deck." Through it all, he lives with the frightening awareness that he must face the dawn of each day with all its problems, chief of which is getting the money to buy the drug.

Listen, kids, the world of dope is not a fantasy world. It is very real. It is also very horrible and very tragic. If you haven't come up against it, good! If, however, some day some guy offers you a new kind of kick and a new kind of cigarette, whistle for the cops.

It would be a very good idea if once in a while you said a prayer for those kids who have already been hooked. Thousands of them are in state hospitals, suffering the pangs of the damned, trying to fight their way back to health and sanity. It is a long, twisting road back. Some of them will make it, but lots of them will get out with one thought in mind — to get just one more "fix," then get off it forever. The result: they will never be cured.

Pray for these kids. They may never have had parents who really cared about them. They fell easy prey to traffickers in dope. They were sold right down the river by everybody. They are pretty much at the end of their rope. Their only release will be six feet of dirt on top of them. By all means avoid it yourself; and pray for those who didn't.

YOU AND YOUR GIRL

CHAPTER SEVENTEEN

Everybody's Getting Married

You can fight it if you want to, but it won't do a bit of good. The world is full of people, and that's all there is to it. All you have to do is climb into your car at the beginning of one of those long weekends and start driving to the lake or the seashore. Everybody in the world is right there on your highway heading for your seashore. It's "antsville."

One hundred and eighty million people are milling around in our vast country and we know it. Of all these people, some are men and some are women. And, if you examine the setup with a very studied vision, one fact will hit you square in the mush — the normal thing for all the people in the world is that they get married.

Everybody's getting married. Walk up and down any street in your town and, believe it, all those houses are sheltering married people. Look down from an airplane at all those homes, those farmhouses, those factories. Married people all over the place.

So for those of you who worry about the future, whether you will find a mate or not, loosen up. It's easy. Anybody can do it. Bunch up with 99 classmates and friends someday and you will now make up a crowd of 100 guys. Before you reach the age of 45, 10 of you will be dead, 5 of you will be in religious life, 5 of you will be bachelors, and 80 of you will be married. So if you want to marry, your chances are pretty good. Don't worry about it.

You do not have to have a magnificent physique to assure yourself of marriage. Girls do not have to have the face of an angel or a velvet complexion; so neither do you men have to look like Rock Hudson or have the muscles of Mickey Hargitay. Appearances are strange things. A girl might look like an empty CARE package, a boy might have a face like a ball of twine, but they will see beauty in each other and they will marry.

This has to be. It is the will of God. It is the work of God. It would *have* to be because only God, in His divine power, could keep the system going. You look at a married man sitting perhaps in a bar on his way home from work and he doesn't have much to say about his wife that is good or beautiful. Occasionally, he will refer to her as his better half, but only in polite society. Sitting here in his favorite pub, with glazed eyes and beer-sodden brain, he refers to her as his warden or his loudspeaker or simply as the "war department."

She, on the other hand, enjoys telling her bridge-playing friends at their weekly get-together what kind of a big clod she married. True, he is her lover, her one and only, and the father of her children; but he is also her pain in the neck.

Why does it have to be like this? Why must marriage be referred to as the battlefield of life. Why has it been the butt of so many jokes? *The Saturday Evening Post* has the whole country yucking over cartoons which depict, with a great deal of accuracy, the incongruities and the foibles of matrimony.

Let's just let it go as a gag. Let's keep our sense of humor. There is something laughable in everything. There are many things laughable in marriage. The really horrible marriage, the big mistake, is relatively rare. The so-called impossible marriage is the result of inexcusable ignorance or selfish, childish nonsense. Ordinarily, with a little humility and a little patience, with a whole lot of love and an intelligent, mature outlook on the whole thing, the average marriage can be a very beautiful and very rewarding experience for any husband and wife.

It has been said that there are worse things than being single and one of them is being married. However, there is little to compare with the union of two people that really works. It radiates beauty. There is little more a man needs than the love of a good wife, the love which he sees in her eyes when he comes home from work each day. That alone is quite enough to turn him into a giant. That alone is quite enough to enable him to shut out the harsh world of men until the next day. And in the morning he will have found in her the strength to go out and cope with his business life once more.

As for a wife; well, maybe it is true (and it is) that women spend billions on beauty aids, but it is not this that makes a woman beautiful. The one fact that makes a woman beautiful is the love of a man. The love of her husband.

For many of you, then, only marriage will make you full persons in this life and great saints in another. Marriage is a must for you. But not marriage to anybody. Marriage to the *right person*. So before you make the big choice, you better be sure you know what you're doing. Such a thing takes much study, much thinking, and much prayer. Remember, the salvation of your immortal soul depends not, primarily, on marriage, but rather on *whom* you lead into marriage.

CHAPTER EIGHTEEN

Morality Makes Sense

I'll tell you one thing, I hate traffic laws. Oh, I guess I hate a lot of things — mustaches, broccoli, hot-air hand driers, and people who are always asking me if I have writer's cramp as I sit autographing books at a literary tea. Yes, I guess I hate a lot of things; but I hate traffic laws best of all.

Red lights make me go into hypnoidal trances; stop signs throw me into catatonic stupors. Every time I see a notice on the side of the road, "25-Mile Speed Limit," I let up on my accelerator and let out on my frustration.

I don't like traffic laws (you probably gathered this by now) but I *do* observe them. And I obey them, not only because I am afraid of that car with the red gum ball machine on its roof but also because I know that if I disregarded them I would become a threat to human life, a killer on wheels, aiming a missile instead of driving a car; and I would hurt myself. Without traffic laws, I would die. And I don't like that idea.

I know something else, too. I know that if our President told us that on the 4th of July, in order to establish again the fact that we are a free people living in a free land, we would not have to observe the traffic laws; that we could blandly disregard the red lights and the stop signs, the speed limits; that we could take left turns from right lanes and right turns from left lanes, make U turns anywhere, go in circles on Main Street — I know one thing for dead certain, I'd stay home. All day long. Nothing would get me out into that American butchery just for the purpose of expressing my freedom. In other words, we don't have to *like* laws, but we do have to recognize our need for them. Without traffic laws, we've had it.

I guess some of you fellows feel the way I do about laws. You dislike laws. OK! Just as long as you do not start disliking the giver of law and the custodian of law. What I'm trying to say is: stop hating authority.

Some of you do, you know. Besides hating hot-air handdriers and other sundry things, you also hate authority. When I was a kid, I actually liked "Clubby," the traffic cop on our corner. Today, who likes cops? They are called "screws," the "fuzz," "headbeaters," "taxeaters," and many other things.

The big danger in hating human laws and human authority is that we might end up hating God's laws and God's authority. God gave us laws for one purpose only. To guide and direct us to the only true and genuine existence, heaven. He did not make laws first and then twist people to fit the laws. He first of all made people. Then He made laws to fit people.

Heaven forbid that we should ever wish to live our lives as if there were no Commandments. Take away the Fifth Commandment and we are all back in the days of Gunsmoke with hair-trigger six-shooters strapped to our legs. Take away the Seventh Commandment and we stand guard over all our property, living in constant fear that somebody will pull the big heist on everything we own. Above all, take away the Sixth Commandment and we move back into the jungle where we proceed to wipe ourselves off the face of the earth.

Arnold Toynbee in his monumental *History of the World* has pointed out that since the beginning of time there have been nineteen distinct civilizations. Of this number, sixteen have destroyed themselves from within. Therefore, the fact remains quite obvious that if we in our own day and within our own civilization hope to survive, then we must maintain a strong and imperishable sense of morality.

Now, this high school courtship scene is a real grabber. What man among you, for instance, will ever forget your high school days? Or your first date? Or maybe your first kiss? These memories will never be lost. And they can be beautiful memories, too. The joyous discovery of every boy who finally wakes up to the fact that girls are not really an accident of creation after all is unforgettable. In high school, companionship with the opposite sex can be the most thrilling experience of a whole lifetime. That is, as long as you play it straight.

But let a fellow and a girl, in their early courtship days, disregard basic laws of human morality and they cut themselves a fair slice of tragedy. They not only jeopardize their own eternal salvation, but they chip surely and devastatingly at the foundation of civilization itself.

Ancient Rome was just about the zenith of man's sojourn on earth. Never before had he risen to such heights of learning and culture. Never had he enjoyed such abundance. Never did he have it so good.

But ancient Rome went soft and let itself fall into the clutches of licentiousness until people who practiced all sorts of debauchery were merely looked upon by the populace as interesting characters. Rome strangled on its own sensuality. If we do not take stock of our own moral lives in this year of our Lord, then I will give you good odds that the glories of a modern America will soon follow the glories of ancient Rome — in corruption, destruction, and oblivion.

There are many things wrong with the world today. It is not necessarily your fault. If you have discovered a trend downward on the part of adults, why complain about it? Your job, in these wonderful years of youth, is to start the trend upward.

CHAPTER NINETEEN

It's Tough to Be Good

Some of you guys might wonder if you will ever be able to run a four-minute mile, and some of your gals might wonder if they will ever be able to bake a gumlash pie (like who can bake a gumlash pie); but none of you need wonder if you will ever fall in love. You will. It is a normal procedure in growing up.

Your love life, like everybody's, develops through five stages. First you love yourself. Then you love your parents. After that, you love your playmates. Then you work up a big crush on someone of your own sex, like a teacher, sports' hero, or a scoutmaster. Finally, as a teen-ager, you develop a keen interest in the opposite sex. That's girls.

Now, if you are a normal kid, your flight through the first four loves is uneventful and quite harmless. It is the fifth love that will expose you, and probably for the first time, to the danger of serious sin. It is a sad fact, but true, that the first mortal sin most young people commit is a sin against purity. Here is a new violent force that explodes upon the erstwhile serene course of your life, and one with which you do not know just how to cope. Finally, you realize that this thing called temptation is no longer that urge to get into the cooky jar or to beat up your sister. This is big. It is for keeps. It sweeps you to the very fringes of life and eternity. It is not, therefore, something to be taken lightly.

What about this new fact of temptation, then? Well, it might seem remotely possible that you could go around say-

ing, "I have no brain"; but you could never go around saying,
"I have no temptations." If you don't have any temptations,
you are in the wrong place. You belong on a slab. If you don't
have any temptations, for heaven's sake, lie down. You're
dead.

Temptations are an essential part of life. They are there
and there isn't one single, solitary thing you can do about
it. No nation, no class, no profession is exempt. Neither is
any individual. Just as surely as there are death, taxes, and
pancake houses, so also there are temptations.

People had them in the second century; they had them in
the tenth. Saints as well as sinners felt their scourge. Even the
butcher, the baker, and the candlestick maker had them; but
not the cow that jumped over the moon. Temptations are
reserved for human beings. So when they come, you can at
least console yourself with the thought that you are human,
if nothing else.

Temptations are commonly considered to be banging out
at us from three sources — the devil, the world, and the flesh.

Take the devil! Now here is a repulsive cat who really hates
you. He hates everything about you, the way you talk and
walk and brush your teeth. His prime interest is dragging you
into hell, hoping to alleviate his own misery by your presence
there. Make no mistake about it. He is quite real. He has been
unable to get through to you in the past; but now, in the days
of your courtship, he is purring over the thought of a rich
harvest.

Then there's the world. The world, so it says, has "grown
up." It has brought sex out into the open in a manner almost
without parallel in history. Generally, teen-agers aren't any
worse today than they were a hundred years ago, or even a
generation ago. It's only that being good today is a bit tougher
than it was when I was a kid.

When I was a kid, there were no such things as drive-
in theaters. We all know about those places. So *there* was

one less temptation. Likewise, when I was a kid, there was no suggestiveness coming into my living room through the medium of television. Nor did we have cars for dating. (I do believe some of you realize that cars are sometimes used for purposes other than mere transportation.) When we went out on a date, we used bicycles. With bicycles, you *have* to be good.

Finally, the flesh. We have all been crippled by the sin of our first parents. It is they who are responsible for the fact that it is always much easier to be bad than to be good. We are all hungry for acceptance. We are all hungry for love. But we must never make the mistake of thinking that sex and sex experiences are the same thing as love.

Therefore, you young men growing up in a positively pagan atmosphere should never be surprised at the presence of temptation in your life. According to a sociologist from Harvard you are exposed to some threat to your purity every seven minutes of your waking day. This is rough. It does not mean that you are less good.

It means that since there are a lot more temptations going around, there are going to have to be a lot more guys with a lot more guts. The remedy is old — the avoidance of the occasion of sin. If you are going to place yourselves repeatedly alone in parked cars (that's an occasion of sin), sooner or later you are going to fail Christ. And when you fail Christ, you alter the map of your destiny.

The only place you will find the strength to rise above all the lowness around you is at the rail. Try Christ in the Blessed Sacrament. He conquered the world, the flesh, and the devil. He can help you do the same.

CHAPTER TWENTY

Concerning Potato Bugs

When you're young you can do a lot of things better than when you're old — especially make mistakes. We older people know this because we have been through it. As a youth, you could develop a hatred for authority. You could become a thief because stealing seems easier than working. You could get yourself involved with alcohol or even narcotics, God forbid. Many, many mistakes you could make; but the worst of all, the kind which you must live with all your life, the kind which leads not to improvement but to trouble, is the mistake of kicking purity out of your life.

"Well, aren't you the stuffy one," some of you might be thinking. "Here we are, practically thrown together in parked cars, and you yell purity. Magazines with their crude advertisements suggest that life isn't life unless it is filled with sex activity. Sex is pleasant; and besides, aren't we supposed to drink of life to the full by trying every new experience? Go back to the Dark Ages, Father, with your blatherings about purity. That word isn't used any more."

Behold, musing youth, I do have big news for you. Yes, I will go back to the Dark Ages with my talk about purity. It was needed then. It is needed no less today. Modern times with modern ideas can never change impurity into purity. What was pure then is still pure; what was impure then is still impure today. Some things are changeless; and this is one of them.

Biologists can look into their microscopes and observe that the whole life cycle of the potato bug has one purpose, the making of more potato bugs. But we cannot take findings that look good in a biology lab and transfer them unchanged to human behavior. We are not potato bugs, and it's a good thing to remember. We are not animals.

When God made animals (and potato bugs) He put them down on all fours, their faces pointed toward the earth, scrounging for food to sustain themselves. But when He made you, He made you straight up with your eyes automatically reaching out for the stars, and toward the heaven which is your real destiny.

To animals God gave instinct; to you He gave intellect and will, and thereby made you just a little bit less than angels. Nothing is more in harmony with the dignity of man than the virtue of purity; nothing more degrading than its opposite. God commanded purity because He loves you. He wants to protect you. In His divine wisdom, He knows that nothing is more harmful, more deadly to the individual or to mankind in general than a cold-blooded, sneering disregard of morality.

So now, as you emerge from the cocoon of childhood and enter onto the threshold of maturity, make sure you adopt a good sound sense of morality for your courtship days. No period in a person's life is quite like this one. The memory of it will never dim through the years but will live on and on. For this reason, memories of courtship days should be only good memories.

It is too bad, indeed, that the dating habits of some kids have taken them into the pits of ugliness where they cease to enjoy life but rather groan beneath the burdens of remorse. It is too bad that in future years their only remembrances of their dating days will be sordid ones.

And when sex enters into dating, it becomes sordid. A guy takes a girl out, buys her a coke (big deal), then tries to squeeze it out of her on the way home. Around every lake, along every river, cars are parked. And there are people in them. And all of them are stupidly riding down the oldest and most deceptive channel in the world. It's just too bad.

Let's make that transition from childhood into young manhood a sparkling beautiful thing. For that is what it should be. When boys are little they think all girls are sissified creeps, and all little girls think that boys are roughneck jerks. Each sex wonders what the other sex is doing on the same earth with them. Some even question the wisdom of God in setting things up the way He did. But, thank heavens, time changes this.

It happened to me in the sixth grade. I was all scootched up in my desk, trying to read a comic book without getting caught, when there was a knock on the door. Sister's pet, sitting in the first seat in the first row, jumped up to answer it (and how we hated that guy). A messenger from the room across the hall came in with a message for Sister. But what a messenger! She was a little blonde from the girl's sixth grade (they kept us in separate cages). I still remember her name. It was Jeannie Chase. I took one look at her and something new came over me. I had an Adam spasm, a brain blast, right there at my desk. In other words, I flipped. This was a girl? Yes, this was a girl! After that, my life was never the same again. I gave up comic books forever.

It is a beautiful thing when a kid wakes up to the fact of an opposite sex. And it is something that must be kept beautiful throughout the span of a whole lifetime. Keep God in your courtship and, later on, you will always have God in your marriage.

CHAPTER TWENTY-ONE

Anyone for "Kissy-Face"?

Like the whole thing is crazy. You're a guy and this beautiful girl pops majestically into your life. Maybe she is sitting across from you in a doctor's office. Or a bus slithers by you, and you look up and see her face framed in the window, your Mona Lisa with the eyes that shoot sparks. But you never even know her name. So you spend your life wondering who she is and where she is. And you hate the thing that keeps you apart — shyness.

It's the same thing with a girl. He comes trundling around the corner, and this tall, muscular, soft-eyed giant, this athletic male, almost knocks her over. He stops, tells her he is sorry, looks in her eyes for what seem to be years, then moves into orbit again. And her heart breaks. Who is he? Where does he live? Why didn't she say something to him? But he is gone, and the reason why she will never know him — shyness.

This is one of the great frustrations of youth. A boy will sit on one side of a room and the girl on the other. He has an inferiority complex. He doesn't think he is handsome. He is not a football hero. So he fears to approach her lest she spurn him, for this would cast him into the depths of humiliation. So he stays where he is. Yet, at the very same time, she is praying that he will stop and say hello to her, that he will ask her for a date. But she can do nothing but wait, for waiting is the warp and woof of every woman's life. Both these kids experience the agony of shyness.

It might surprise some of you to know that normal shyness

is far more a blessing than a tragedy. If kids never experienced the repressing force of shyness, they would be bunching up and getting married when they are twelve. You can't live with the opposite sex until you learn to live with your own sex. So nature uses a normal amount of shyness to develop normal growth in youth.

If you are shy, don't give up on the world. Shyness is something quite temporary. In time it disappears, and good riddance to it. It is replaced by a normal facility to meet and live and talk with members of the opposite sex.

Now the big act begins. He is always trying to impress her by his wit, his clever repartee, his athletic prowess. He is not really as great as all this, but he tries to make her believe it. She, on the other hand, is also part of the big act. If nature won't give her the kind of figure she wants, Gimbels will. She uses powder and paint, eye shadow and eyebrow pencil so that she will look like what she isn't but much better. It's the big show and the actors take their place upon the stage.

This driving urge to be acceptable to the opposite sex leads, naturally, into this business of affection and its various outward manifestations. You men have heard all about this, but you never seem to tire of the subject. Time and again priests are asked directly and through the anonymous medium of "The Question Box," "Just what's with the kiss? Is it right or wrong? Can you kiss before, during, or after a date? Do you kiss after one date? Or ten? Or what? How long can it last? Ten seconds? Twenty?" The whole thing gets pretty well smogged up. Let's try to clarify it.

First of all, a kiss, in itself, is not something evil, dirty, or sinful. If you get a medal in the French army, you get a couple of kisses with it. Gagarin got kissed by Khrushchev for orbiting the earth. If you win the Indianapolis "500," you get kissed by a beautiful girl. Nimble Irishmen, as well as tourists visiting Ireland, do backflips to kiss the Blarney Stone. You get a hundred days' indulgence every time you kiss a bishop's ring. We kiss our parents because we love them. Little kids get kissed on the top of their head by adults; old men get kissed on the top of their bald heads by little girls. Eskimos, as we all know, kiss by rubbing noses (although I'm sure I don't know why). What I am trying to say is that there is a lot of kissing going on, and not all of it is evil.

But then there are kisses and there are kisses. The first time kids kiss, it is a very tentative, shy, quick little peck, then run. Later, a little warmth is added and this is the "I like you and hope you like me" kiss. But things start going sour when you come up with the "I like to kiss you and I want to kiss you more and more" kiss. When a kiss becomes a trigger for sexual gratification, outside of marriage, then it is way out and sinful.

Therefore, a deeply passionate kiss for unmarried people is always sinful. And please don't give us the old guff about a kiss not bothering you. If you are human, then every time you kiss at length, whether you believe it or not, your heartbeat is stepped up, your pores are opened, your pituitary gland goes into action, triggering other glands and preparing the body for further action. This happens to all people.

Then there is the problem of the car, and I do call it a problem. Kids who own cars invariably get the worst marks in school, and that is bad. But cars, too, have contributed mightily to the moral decadence of youth. When you play "kissy-face" in parked cars, you can be sure that there is nothing right about it. Such close and prolonged and uninterrupted proximity can only create serious problems. Necking is wrong, and I am sorry.

Being creatures of intelligence, you must always be on guard against these attractive sins that can only hurt you in the end; and you must, at all times, be true to your conscience. The general principle for conduct is: It is a mortal sin for unmarried persons to seek deliberate sexual pleasure, either partial or complete. It may seem a bit hard. But there it is.

CHAPTER TWENTY-TWO

Your Teen-Age World of Don't

It is pretty obvious that teen-agers today are being don'ted to death. But so are we all. Don't pick the flowers. Don't walk on the grass. Don't smoke in the "johns." Don't feed the animals. Don't swim in shark-infested waters. Don't eat the daisies. Don't be a nut. And so forth and so on, forever and ever. Amen.

This is natural because it is a lot easier to tell people what they can't do than to tell them what they can. Telling people what they *can* do takes brains.

So here are a few more don'ts for your collection. And we offer them with the hope that they will help you make the proper choice in the choice of all choices — of a marriage partner.

First of all don't marry a girl if she intends spending the rest of her life working in the business world. This means that you will get yourself a half wife and a half mother. Not only is being a housewife a full-time job, but if you get used to two paychecks you are headed for trouble. When she must stop working and her paycheck stops coming in, you will not be able to live up to the standard you set for yourselves. Either you try staying up there and get ulcers for your efforts, or you come down a notch. Both situations are almost impossible. If you cannot support the girl you marry, then you have no business getting married to her.

Don't marry a girl who hates her home. She will hate your

home too. She will hate housework and she will probably hate children. It's a queer duck of a woman who hates kids; and brother, you married her.

Don't marry a girl who does not have a sense of humor. Her beautiful body will grow wrinkles, but never her laughter.

By the same token, no girl will marry you if you need reforming. If you're lazy, irresponsible, and shiftless now, you will be the same after the ceremony. She won't change you. Further, a girl will never marry you if you're jealous and suspicious. Because as long as she lives, you will be firmly convinced that she is carrying on with every salesman who comes to her door, and she knows this. Or she should. The Sacred Scripture says, "A jealous man or woman is the grief and mourning of the heart."

In general, marriage is dangerous if your in-laws can't get along at all. Don't kid yourselves. Your girl's family comes right along in the deal. And, of course, if you take up house-keeping in the home of your parents, or hers, right away you are dead.

Please don't marry just to escape a difficult home situation. Marriage is not an escape. The thing to do is to measure up to the challenge, solve it one way or the other, then move out. And here is something else. Don't marry too hastily a girl whose family has a tradition of divorce. Step very carefully here. Repeated divorces in a family might point up to an inherent sense of instability.

Don't marry an alcoholic. Some girls, if we can judge from the way they are always getting juiced, are well on their way to alcoholism. The only thing worse than being an alcoholic is being married to one.

Finally, the big Don't and probably the most important of all is: Don't get entangled in a mixed marriage unless you are completely aware of the challenges that face you. Marriage within one's faith does not automatically guarantee a perfect match; but marriage outside one's faith, the spirit of

Ecumenism notwithstanding, can easily create dangerous ten-
sions that will seriously weaken the bond of marriage itself.
Intelligent, understanding, mature individuals can indeed make
a mixed-marriage work; but not everybody can always be
intelligent, understanding, and mature.

The reason is obvious. Social differences can be remedied
by orientation; educational differences, by study. But religious
differences only create a chasm that widens and deepens
through the years. Marriage is supposed to be a union, a
oneness. Without this oneness there can never be a really perfect marriage. It is a oneness not only of body and heart
and soul, but also of mind; and people of different religions
will never achieve oneness of mind. They may tolerate each
other's religion — but what kind of a marriage is it if the
best you can offer is tolerance?

I'm sure I never met a young couple, entering a mixed
marriage, who did not say, "But Father, our case is different.
We understand each other perfectly in this matter of religion
and we are not going to let it interfere with our marriage."
Whether they like it or not, religion *will* interfere. It is too
big not to, it is too vast to be overlooked. Religion reaches out
into the trackless stretches of eternity. You can't just push it
out of the way. It *must* be considered.

Mixed marriages are not worth the risk. One survey reveals
that 75 per cent of them end up in divorce or separation.

Just because I am taking shots at mixed marriages does
not mean that I am taking shots at non-Catholics. It is just
as important for non-Catholics to marry non-Catholics as
it is for Catholics to marry Catholics. It is not a question here
of one being better than the other. It is *not* a question of
morality. It is a question of belief.

A husband and wife who have different creeds and beliefs
will always be at odds on the question of divorce. To one it
is forbidden; to the other it is permissible. A couple such as
this will also run into dead ends in the matter of birth control.

They will constantly be in disagreement as to just how the children should be brought up, what church they should be sent to, what they should be taught; and the poor kids are in the middle of this mess and don't know just what direction is up.

It takes many things to make a marriage (sacrifices of all shapes and sizes); it takes only one chink to tear a marriage apart, and a difference of religion, more than anything else, is the first chink that starts the disintegration. Marriage lasts for a whole lifetime. There is no second chance. It is for keeps. So don't take any unnecessary risks. Love everybody. Respect the convictions and the beliefs of your non-Catholic and non-Christian fellow men. Participate with a full heart in inter-denominational fellowship with others of different creeds. But when you marry, marry one of your own. It will make your chances a little bit better.

CHAPTER TWENTY-THREE

Play It Loose

I am going to start off this chapter with a quotation. So get ready. Here it is. "Nothing like the young people of today has ever been seen. They make one's hair stand on end. They have neither manners nor morals."

Right away you scream because you've heard all that before. You're sick of adults who are always knocking your teen-age world. But the interesting thing about my opening quotation is that it is *not* modern. As a matter of fact it's pretty old. It was written back in 1817.

Therefore I hope you guys will never take too seriously the open charges you hear that this generation is all kooky. In every age adults think that teen-agers are the worst that ever existed. Why, in twenty years, when some teen-age boy throws a rock through a church window, you will say, "That's it. That's the end. We'll never survive." This is a fact. Even in the ruins of Babylon a cuniform fragment was discovered on which was inscribed, "Alas, times are not what they used to be." And that was 2225 B.C.

For this reason, I don't get upset over all the new dance crazes that come down the path. I don't think the reactions of youth toward the Beatles, the Hermits, the Rolling Stones, and all the other combos like them signal the end of the world and the deterioration of youth. For there is nothing new about fads, and nothing new about hero worship.

Take Franz Liszt, for instance. He was a great Hungarian

virtuoso. That means he was a good musician. He could really blow a piano. A lot of kids would lose their cookies if they had to sit and listen to him, but in his own time he was the rage. When teen-age girls attended his concerts back in 1825, they smuggled in scissors, vaulted upon the stage, and chopped off locks of his hair. A wonder he didn't get his eye squished out. The water in which he washed his hands was bottled and sold to his endearing fans. His cigar butts were worn in lockets around the necks of his female followers. It proves one thing: that the teen-agers a hundred years ago were pretty kook, too. So we can't say that a girl who wears her boyfriend's shoehorn around her neck is any nuttier today than the girls in the past century.

There is, however, something in our day that did not exist among teen-agers in the past. It is the code and the custom of going steady, and no matter how you look at it or what you say about it, the thing is real bad berries. I have been taking shots at this for a long time and I don't seem to be getting through. I'm about ready to throw in the spongerino. Reason doesn't seem to work; threats are useless. The sad experiences that have resulted from this are blithely shrugged off by teen-agers who say, "My case is different." So what's a guy do?

It takes a lot of things to make a good marriage, and maybe you are working at them all. But just as soon as you get involved in this deadly game of going steady without any thought of marriage, then you are cutting your legs right out from under you. You can argue all you want about the pros and cons of this caper, but it is a giant mistake, the whole thing, and it is too bad that so many of you get suckered into this jazz.

What's so wrong about it? Well, first of all, the system is fraught with dangers to your purity. In the course of my priestly work, I have come in contact with the young unwed mother, and there are many of these unfortunate girls around.

Last year two hundred thousand unmarried girls brought children into this world, and that is a tragedy. I don't know about all those two hundred thousand girls, but everyone of those who came to me was going steady. Nature doesn't change; it always works the same way. The longer a guy and a girl are together, the more they get used to each other. This initiates certain familiarities which create a situation in which things get cozier and cozier. With all this comes a certain blindness that makes them both think they need each other for the rest of their life. Then their spiritual life goes to pot because they start rationalizing: "This can't be evil. We are in love." It is all downhill, the whole thing. Kids who are going steady for a long time are pretty much baring their tattered souls to the world. It is all too human.

Now the Church is against anything that will jeopardize the salvation of your soul. So this moral problem in going steady is a primary consideration. But the Church is also concerned about your earthly happiness, and in the long run, going steady will lessen your chances for earthly happiness. Kids who go steady through high school usually end up getting married right after graduation. So here's another big blunder. When you marry at this age, you destroy the freedom that would normally become yours at this period of your life. You will lose out on your best years. You will be sitting up all night, at the age of nineteen trying to keep a bigmouthed baby quiet, while your classmates, who saved all year at their job, are spending two weeks on the beaches of Miami or Waikiki. For you there is no excitement or travel but only the grave responsibilities of married life. You owe it to yourself to enjoy the freedom of youth. You are out of your mind when you saddle yourself with obligations that go along with marriage. Remember, marriage might have its privileges, but the obligations are far more numerous.

And here is something else. Early marriage means an end to education. Not always, but most of the time. In these days, to really keep up, a college degree is almost an absolute must. "You've got each other. Your love will make all things possible!" I'm sorry, but it won't.

To sum up, going steady is a threat to your morality. Going steady always precedes early marriages. And early marriages are the ones most likely to fail. A teen-ager who marries has three times as many chances of failing as one who marries at the age of twenty-one.

The custom of steady company keeping cannot be destroyed by the Church or by parents; it has to be destroyed by teen-agers. It is a question of being courageous enough to be a nonconformist. We can't offer you anything in return but the promise of a better life later on. And you will have to take our word on that. Don't shackle yourself so early in life. Move around more. Meet different people. Play the game loose.

CHAPTER TWENTY-FOUR

Holy Enough for Marriage

Let's say that you have just about made up your mind about your future. You had been told about the three possible vocations and you were conscientious enough to examine them.

You heard about the vocation of the unmarried person living in the world. You were shown how a person could dedicate his life to God without going into a seminary. But you didn't like the overall picture. A vocation like this, you figured, had neither the spiritual consolations of religious life nor the physical consolations of married life. You scratched it off the list.

Then you took a good look at religious life. You found a massive challenge here. You were informed that over half the people on the face of the earth have still not received the good tidings of the Gospels. They have never heard about Christ. And if they formed a line that would pass by you so that you could hand them some little pamphlet about Christ, you would stand there handing out literature for forty-five years. You were told about the priest in Idaho who has a parish that covers an area of 30,000 square miles and no one to help him. You came finally to the frightening, discouraging realization that, with the manpower we presently have in the Church, it is a physical impossibility to bring the world back to Christ. You have considered the magical, magnificent invitation, "Come, follow Me." But all the same, you have crossed this off your list. You are not against it, of course. You are not against the missionary toting his Mass

kit through the jungles of the Philippines. You are not against
the priest living his life in a truck as he travels through the
bush country of Australia. And you are not against the nun
binding the repulsive sores of the leper. But it is not for you,
you say. And if you have given this possible vocation much
prayerful thought, much examination, then we must go along
with you in your decision.

So now you have eliminated two of three possibilities. For
you, then, there is only one possibility left. Marriage. And
this, you honestly believe, is the vocation that Christ expects
you to follow. The only question left now is, "Do I know what
I am getting into? Do I understand this vocation — its privileges and obligations?"

The first question you must answer is: Am I old enough?
Validly and legally, you can be married when you are sixteen.
But is this old enough? Absolutely not. Neither is eighteen old
enough. Divorce courts these days are filled with teen-agers.
They thought they were old enough, but maturity is not
counted in years. Teen-age marriages are too often built on
the sand dunes of emotion. They fall apart easily.

Another question you must face: Am I skilled enough? It
is a sad plight indeed that today one has less trouble getting
a marriage license than he has getting a driver's license.
To some people this probably means that driving a car is
harder and takes more ability than running a marriage. This
is the heresy of all heresies. What comes over you kids when
you think that being a husband is a natural thing needing no
preparation or training at all? Some young men have the
audacity to approach marriage without knowing the funda-
mentals in the use of tools. They know nothing about painting
a house. They are completely ignorant of basic finances. They
think that all you need for a successful marriage is a car,
TV set, and each other. Some girls are no different. A girl
will embrace marriage thinking a spatula is a new kind of
pizza. She does not have the slightest awareness of the art

of cooking. Her greatest contribution to her marriage is that she is a good dancer.

Any young people contemplating marriage must ask themselves, will I be able to do, right now, exactly what my mother or father can do? Could I step into their shoes? Do I have the kind of education that will enable me to provide for a family? Do I have the knack of sewing and making clothes for my children because they will be too expensive to buy? In other words, do I have the moxie for marriage?

The third question is: Am I holy enough? Don't make any mistake about this. You might have excluded yourself from the religious life on the grounds that you were not holy enough to be a priest. But get it straight. If you are not holy enough to be a priest, what makes you think you are holy enough to get married? A good successful marriage will demand all the basic elements of spirituality. To be a success in married life, as a matter of fact, you will almost have to be a saint, because only a saint could fulfill perfectly all the demands and the challenges of matrimony. If you are not holy at all, then you better start looking for a fourth vocation. You don't fit in any of the others.

If teen-agers are going to approach the consideration of marriage with any degree of intelligence, they must remember that it is primarily a Sacrament. Christ thought so highly of Matrimony that He besparkled it with exalted dignity. But do not mistake the motives of Christ. He did not make marriage a Sacrament so that some empty-headed bride would be able to buy a very expensive gown with a ridiculously long train that would have her floundering and tripping up the sanctuary steps. Nor did Christ make marriage a Sacrament so that during the wedding ceremony some soprano could warble, "Because" or "I Love You Truly." Christ was not thinking about bridal gowns and soloists when He so divinely dignified the union of man and woman. But He did cover this union with blessedness so that a husband and wife, brought together in His name, might begin to make something other than themselves, and, in their moments of holy love, become a lord and lady of life and creation itself.

Matrimony is no wild gig. It is not a perpetual hayride. It is not floating off in a pretty, pink bark of bliss. It is not many things. But it is a Sacrament. Any bride or groom must be aware of its sacred character. And its sacredness goes on and on; only death can destroy the marriage bond. It demands of a man and woman that they live out their lives together and in holiness.

Marriage is holy; it is also hard. So if you are not willing to make sacrifices and if you are not interested in loving God more, then you might just as well try something else.

CHAPTER TWENTY-FIVE

With This Ring . . .

This is your wedding day and a great new world spreads itself out before you. You stand in the church waiting for the organ to open up with the first chords of your wedding march. Your heart is full. You are anxious, a wee bit afraid; your stomach is full of flusters, and every once in a while, by way of reassuring yourself, you say, "Surely, this is God's will. This is what He wants of me."

And it is. You have chosen a life partner who is pretty much your equal. You have a common intellectual bond, come from the same kind of family, like pretty much the same things, and share a common faith. You have always kept God in your courtship, so now on your wedding day, He leads you both to your common destiny. There is no reason for worry. The organ sounds and you move to meet your lover before the altar of God where you will join your hearts and souls in a union so sacred and intimate as to affect your whole life. The quest is over; your life's work begins.

Your wedding ceremony will be more of a dream to you than the reality which it is. You will be caught up, carried aloft in the holy pageantry of your nuptial Mass. You will pronounce your vows to each other and then, hardly believing it is all real, you will start the return march to the church door. Your friends will watch you as they smile or snivel in their pews, and your heart will be bursting with joy. You will have your reception in the evening and then, with everybody just a little bit high, you will find a propitious moment to spirit each other away from the festivities and into the future. Now you are really Mr. and Mrs.

We know how Elizabeth Barrett Browning felt about her husband when we read her beautiful, "How have I loved thee — let me count the ways." And we understand how Winston Churchill felt about his wife when we read, "My marriage was much the most fortunate and joyous event which happened to me in the whole of my life; for what can be more glorious than to be united in one's walk through life with a being incapable of an ignoble thought."

Indeed, marriage has been called an ecstasy. It has been called a slavery. But somewhere in between, it is a normal state of life in which two people, by sanctifying each other, ultimately sanctify themselves. It is a life that in its barest minimum demands great love, for only such love can make it work. It presupposes a close understanding, because only a compassionate understanding can make the difference between success and failure when a husband wakes up to the fact that his wife is a woman and she realizes that her husband is a man.

Rarely have the sexes ever been able to understand each other. A husband will never understand why his wife complains about the lack of closet space in the house and then bemoans the fact that she has nothing to wear. He will never understand why she spends two hours in the backyard telling the lady next door that she never has time to get her housework done. Nor will he ever understand why his wife will have the plumber in the house all morning, and have coffee and toast too, alone, together; then become livid with rage when she finds out that he took his secretary to lunch in front of four hundred people. A man must learn to accept these things from his wife.

On the other side, a woman will wonder why her husband refuses to say, "I'm sorry," because she fails to understand that one of the hardest things a husband must do, even when he knows he's wrong, is to say "I'm sorry." She must understand that her husband loves her even if he never comes out and says it. A man expects his wife to know this. He shouldn't, of course. He should *tell* his wife of his love, but he doesn't, and that is that. Married people must learn to live with the oddities of each other. These quirks cannot be made the hinges upon which a marriage works. They are much too small for that.

You have heard it said time and time again that the primary purpose of marriage is the raising and educating of children, while the secondary purpose (but equally important) is the fostering of love between husband and wife. Love will come easily; but if married couples cannot figure children into their marriage, then they better not even figure marriage. It is the child who gives meaning to marital love. Couples can speak of their love for each other; but only when a child scampers across the living-room floor are they able to look at each other and say, "This is the living, breathing proof of how much I love you."

You hear a lot of babblery these days about the population explosion and the spacing of children, comments such as, "We are going to have our children after we get the house paid for, or the TV set, or the car." But it is a sad indictment to a marriage when a child must play second fiddle to all these other baubles. It will be well for you to remember that an unborn child does not care what kind of a house he lives in or what kind of a car his father drives. These are unimportant to him. The only thing an unborn child wants — and as his parents, you could be the only ones to give it to him — is life. He just wants to live. And when you give him earthly existence, you almost give him eternal existence.

Children bring fulfillment to marriage that nothing else can bring. Abysmally distorted is the reasoning of couples who look upon children as an intrusion into their love. Love that can be weakened by children could not have been love in the first place. Children are the very cement of married life.

Within the home of a large family in Ohio there hangs on the kitchen wall a sign which reads, "This home was built for and because of children; they shall not be denied herein." This makes sense to me.

If, in future years, the problems of married life wear heavily upon you, remember what was read to you on your wedding day: "Only love will make it easy, and perfect love will make it a joy."

Conclusion

We only hope, as you go your merry way through life, that you will never forget the responsibility resting on your shoulders. You're important to God. So important, in fact, that rather than create new angels to spread His teachings throughout the world, He created you.

And although you might beg off from the challenge by saying that you are not very intelligent or not very holy, you must not forget that when Christ chose to put His Church into the hands of a human being, He did not pick the very scholarly Paul, or the very mystical John, but the very, human, fumbling, weak, ordinary Peter. He still does. You must walk in the knowledge that God will use you every day to lead others to Him. It might be in many little ways and under many different circumstances, but use you He will.

Therefore, men, it would seem to be most imperative that the example you set is of the highest and finest type. Lead the world upward, not downward. People will pass through your life with souls more precious than the king's ransom. What a tragedy it would be if, instead of bringing them closer to God, you led them farther away.

So get with it. Take the measure of yourselves and the world around you. You are little; the world is big. And there is so much wrong with the world. But God made an imperfect world, and He did it deliberately, so that you by your manliness and your purity and your love might add your finest touch to His great masterpiece.

•